NO SHIT!
THERE I WAS...

*wild stories
from wild people*

NO SHIT!
THERE I WAS...
wild stories
from wild people

By Michael Hodgson

Contributing Editor

The Globe Pequot Press

Guilford, Connecticut

Library of Congress Cataloging-in-Publication Data

No shit! There I was—: wild stories from wild people/by Michael Hodgson, contributing editor.
  p. cm.
  Includes index.
  ISBN 0-934802-97-1 :
  1. Adventure and adventurers. I. Hodgson, Michael.

G525.N54 1994
904—dc20   94-49346
                                            CIP

Manufactured in the United States of America
First Edition/Ninth Printing

Table of Contents

Foreword

Nobody ever expects the Skinner Inquisition! In my early youth growing up on a ranch in the Wind River Mountains, I became known for heavy handed questioning of strangers concerning epics they had survived. I realized fully that no man can go everywhere; no man has enough days to see all things. I also realized that I could share in the "reality" of a finely told story and hear, see, feel, and be afraid of things I would never witness. As a young Cowboy, I worked to travel as widely and to experience as much as each day would allow and to hear as many tales as each night could provide.

I've adventured through 25 countries since then. I've climbed sea cliffs in Ireland, Vietnam, Greece and Wyoming. I've been arrested in third world countries like Egypt and Texas. I've starved along side of Rick Ridgeway at the headwaters of the Amazon and climbed to the beat of Zulu drums in Natal. I've eaten turtle eggs, snake, dog, alligator, crocodile, monkey, ostrich, camel, piranha, and horse. I've seen the sun set on the Black, China, Red, and Dead Seas and I've been unable to understand locals in Finland, Poland, Swaziland, and England. All of my memories serve to keep me awake at night thinking of all the things I haven't seen and praying to meet strangers to interrogate about adventures I would never share. As they say back in Wyoming, a good hand and a good story-teller are welcome at any campfire!

Todd Skinner

Introduction

World adventurer and kayaker extraordinair Reg Lake once opined that the major difference between a fairy tale and white water story is that fairy tales begin with, "Once upon a time..." while white water stories always seem to start with "No shit! there I was ... "

Of course, mild or even wildly enhanced exaggeration is by no means the exclusive domain of the white water raconteur. Any outdoorperson, armchair or otherwise, has learned that tall tales are the stuff legends are made of, the meat of glory and the marrow of adventure.

For centuries, while gathered around campfires or smoky watering holes that smell of beer and musty wood, adventurers the world over have regaled all who will listen in that time honored tradition of recounting unbelievable stories that more often than not begin with, "No shit! there I was..." or some other reasonable facsimile. Exaggeration within moderation is key. Humor becomes important, although not essential. Elements of the unbelievable are a must.

I must have heard nearly a million such stories during all the years I have spent outdoors—both as a professional guide and an outdoor writer. A number of these stories get handed down from storyteller to storyteller. An even greater number are pure originals, gaining notoriety as much for the teller's art of verbally recounting the event with humor and skill as for the event itself.

Truly great taletellers have the rare ability to make mountains out of molehills if you give them half a chance. A mere sprained ankle on a weekend backpack can turn into an epic event of biblical proportions, bringing smiles and head shakes of disbelief from the listeners when the lips of the skilled spinner of yarns crafts the tale. Yet, too many of these narrations never get shared beyond the realm of the campsite—disappearing come morning like the dying embers of an evening's fire that once coaxed forth story after story.

It is with the above in mind that I set out to begin placing some of these adventure narratives between the covers of a book for all to enjoy—day in and day out. ICS Books and I created a writing contest, seeking the very best "No Shit! There I Was" accounts the world was willing to share. Stories arrived from all parts of the country. I selected the best of these, some from professional writers, some not, all of which now appear in the following pages, published for your enjoyment. For obvious reasons, my two stories which are included in this book were not entered into the contest—had I won, could you imagine the scandal? That would be a No Shit story in itself.

My congratulations to grand prize winner John Long and runner-up Paul McHugh. Both delivered excellent and entertaining stories.

I am sure that everyone will have a favorite tale or two tucked in between the pages within. I know I've got mine, and I read them over and over, as I am sure you will too. In the meantime, maybe you've got a tale to tell? I hope so, because as you are reading this, ICS Books and I are already seeking more tales of unbelievable proportions for my next book *No Shit! There I Was ... Again!*

Read on and enjoy. Then, if you do have a tale to share and think you have the right stuff to make into these pages for storytelling posterity, read the contest criteria in the back of the book and send away for your official entry form.

Scorched Earth

By: John Long

For two days our situation was critical. Then it got desperate. Our teammates were far ahead, and we needed them. That morning, Rick was a little dizzy and hiking slowly, but we'd sent the others on because we were a week late in finding the next village. No one could have predicted that an hour after they had left us, Rick's symptoms would worsen from dizziness and chills to vomiting and delirium. I pulled him to his feet and we staggered on, wishing we'd never heard of Borneo, of the jungle, of any of it.

We wound through the contours of a luxuriant ravine. Proboscis monkeys screeched high overhead as orange birds shot between towering banyans. The canopy thickened with each step, screening the hot rain that fell in a misty curtain through the hazy green light. The humidity was so thick we exhaled absolute fog. Recent quakes had triggered landslides throughout the rolling terrain, and twice we forded steaming tongues of red mud that flowed over the trail—hip-deep at times—to pick up the track farther on.

Rick Ridgeway and I were two members of a six-man team attempting the first coast-to-coast traverse of Kalimantan, or Indonesian Borneo, a place that time—and everything else—had forgotten, where our native Dyak porters lived as their ancestors did centuries ago. We were thirty-two days out—about halfway across, we hoped,

1

though the government topographic maps showed a huge blank in the jungled interior. I couldn't imagine a lonelier place to get sick.

Rick slumped back on a clump of cane leaves and I bashed down to a little creek to get water, wondering what so quickly could have reduced a veteran of K2 and Everest to a shaking, staggering ruin. Dengue, perhaps. Three years before, in the Solomon Islands, I'd seen an entire German sea kayaking group with dengue fever. It'd resembled a scene from *Night of the Living Dead*. I hoped I was wrong about Rick, but what else could make a man shake like that?

Since leaving the swift Bonai river five days back, we'd thrashed from one Dyak village to the next, linking them with Dyak porters from the former settlement. Most "villages" were no more than clusters of thatched lean-tos, abandoned when the rains stopped and hellacious heat drove the natives into cooler jungle nooks. The next village—Mahak—was supposedly a large one. We couldn't find it. None of our porters had ever been there. But that morning, we'd encountered a band of nomadic Punan Dyaks who said we should have gained Mahak fifteen miles ago.

We continued through the mud, the thorns, the wasps and the leeches. For Rick, staggering through the creepers with a raging fever, every step was a mile. Late that afternoon I wondered if we weren't groping around in a big, tangled circle.

As we broke into a slash-and-burn agricultural swath hacked from a square mile of primal bush, it grew so smoky we could barely see fifty feet. The fuming expanse looked like Hell with the flames turned low. All flora had been felled and torched, to be cleared later for rice fields. Ironwood trees burn slowly, so the blaze lasts for months—never a forest fire, but never quite out. The air, thick and suffocating, was so hot it seemed the very sky was melting. A world-class mountaineer, Rick knew about adversity, but heat, smoke and exhaustion had boosted his fever, and he collapsed at the edge of the clearing.

I winced at the thought of bivouacking and started pacing. Then I found a note tacked on a cannonball tree at trail's edge. The rest of the team, the message ran, had met a Dyak from Mahak who assured them the village was only an hour away. Though wasted from the previous twenty miles, they had pressed on, urging us to follow before nightfall. The red sun hung just above the trees like an open wound. We didn't have much time. The only trail wound straight into the smoke.

During the past four hours, Rick had managed to stumble only a hundred yards at a go, shaking, retching and wheezing. I knew we somehow had to get on with it or the whole, crazy safari was going to end for him right there. I told him this, and he instantly struggled to his feet, ready to march on. I had no idea how far he could go, but I couldn't consider getting stranded in the oven before us. We had to push on.

The trail was distinct for a hundred yards. Then the terrain started rolling, and the path disappeared. The only possible route followed a slanting and broken chain of big trunks spanning a sea of red-hot coals. My eyes streamed from the smoke and my nose filled with the copper stench of the hair singeing off my legs. The setting sun cloaked the clearing in an orange veil, and the course grew doubly confusing. We couldn't pause, even for a second, without burning our feet—even through our boots. The temperature soared and the chain of trunks rose higher above the ground, more disconnected, yet overlaid with wobbly charred saplings that might be the way. And might not. Rick was dead on his feet but continued to wheedle on. He had to. Blue flames leapt from the gutted ironwood trunks that flanked us everywhere. My body poured sweat and I struggled with the urge to ditch Rick and run for my life. But run where? I wondered what the others had done, what route they had followed.

Just ahead, a fifty-foot smoldering ramin trunk—charred halfway through—bowed across a channel of waist-deep coals. The air rippled from the heat rushing off the red embers. We couldn't stop and we couldn't turn back, so I cast off before I analyzed things, my eyes riveted on the far end of that narrow trunk, shimmering in the smoke. About halfway out, the trunk shifted ever so slightly. My hands shot out for balance and sweat popped off the coals below. For a moment I froze, waiting for the trunk to settle in. There was no way I would fall off, but if the bastard snapped, I was gone. Breathing hot little breaths, I tiptoed on until just shy of the cantilevered end. The trunk made a sharp cracking sound. I panicked, lurched forward and sprung off the end onto a hot little knoll.

I kept shifting from one foot to the other, feeling wretched for having led Rick into no-man's land. I couldn't imagine him traversing that trunk, not in his shape. Like he had on so much of this torturous, jackass, extraordinary expedition, he'd have to try because he had no choice. I could hear his reedy breathing from fifty feet away. I thought about going back and helping him, but the trunk was too thin and too charred. We traded sorry looks. He started across.

Arms flailing, he looked like a drunk on a balance beam, but his feet kept shuffling along. Then the trunk started making those horrible cracking sounds, and Rick's feet were skating all over the place and I looked away because I couldn't watch him pitch into the coals, 20 feet below him. When I finally looked back, he was close to the end. But he started getting woozy, sucking each breath and looking bone white and finished. He'd extend his foot like an antenna, rock onto it, wobble, then repeat the move again. I was gnashing my teeth and yelling, "Steady, man, you've got it," fully expecting him to plummet. He wobbled all the last few steps and I screamed, "Jump, man, you've got to jump!" But it wasn't in him. He grimaced, groaned, then half-fell, half-hopped towards me. I grabbed his arm, pulled and we tumbled back, rolling up with big watery blisters on our arms and legs.

Rick draped both arms over my shoulders and I plowed through shallow embers to the edge of the fire, a hundred feet beyond. Amazingly, we straightway ran into a little creek. I toppled in and drank with huge, savage gulps. Then I laid my head on the bank and went out for awhile. When I came around, rain beat down from one black cloud, the blood red moon beside it. A great steamy nimbus welled off the clearing just behind us.

Rick, at the brink of human endurance, still wanted to push on, to get it over with. His fever had first struck while dragging dugout canoes up shallow white water, five days back. Since then, he'd fought through two twelve-hour jungle tromps. And now it was dark and pouring and he wanted to push on. I couldn't figure out what kept him going. Probably Mahak, which we thought had to be close.

It was not.

The squall passed and we trudged a half-hour through stalks of steaming sugarcane that hedged the dark trail, now lit by the moon and the swarms of fireflies that follow every rain. We'd been going for sixteen hours. We stopped. Rick breathed in hideous gasps. Whatever had him, had him good.

Off again. We rounded a corner and there it was: A 600-foot longhouse with dozens of natives huddled around our teammates on the veranda. Everyone had burns and blisters. One of our team-mate's tennis shoes had melted on his foot, and when he'd peeled it off, off came the skin. Yet everyone jumped up and helped Rick into the Chief's room. Clad only in briefs, his mouth a blood-bin of betel nut, the Chief rolled out a rattan mat and Rick collapsed. We tried to rehydrate him, but nothing would stay down and we were helpless to do anything but watch him writhe at our feet, more dead than alive. As fluids ebbed out of him from both ends, his limbs slowly enfolded and his torso curled into a shriveled fetal form terrible to witness. His hours were numbered, but we were astounded to hear that Mahak had a seldom-used grass airstrip and that a missionary pilot from the coast was scheduled to visit the next day. The Chief warned that, though the missionary pilot's word was gold, his puny, single-engined Cessna was often thwarted by coastal squalls.

The plane's echo volleyed through the haze the next morning. Rick, a mere wraith by now, was given priority over sacks of rice and sugar, and the missionary volunteered to take him to his home, since there were no proper hospitals, even on the coast. But the oil companies maintained clinics which, the pilot believed, would accept outsiders with green money. We bid Rick good-bye, and as he arced into the clouds, we were left hanging. None of us really believed he was going to make it. Were we next?

For forty-two days we had motored up the Kapaus river, slow and wide, had bashed and poled up a tributary, swift and rocky, had slashed over the continental divide, an incomprehensible brawl of ripe, primal jungle, had tracked another river to literally drag the dugouts up its last reaches, only to wander around triple canopy jungle for days before finally gaining Mahak. That worked out to about five-hundred miles as the crow flies; but with all the tortured paths and twisting rivers, we figured to have covered about three times that distance. From Mahak, we reckoned the worst was behind us, for only a brief march separated us from the headwaters of the Kayan river and a straight shot to the coast, still two-hundred miles away.

The "brief" march to the Kayan took a week and was the toughest terrain we'd encountered. The Kayan ran smooth for a hundred miles, then narrowed to a fleet gauntlet of raging white water we finally had to quit after flipping twice and loosing one raft altogether. Twenty-one days after leaving Mahak, we were back in the jungle for an eighteen-mile hump around suicidal rapids, were starving and punctured, our ribs standing out like keys on a xylophone. Once out from under the dense canopy of trees and barbed vines, the sun fried us alive as we charged down steaming white water below the portage.

Tanjun Sellor, the first civilized settlement we'd seen in months, looked like El Dorado but for the equatorial swelter. Christ, how could people live in such stupefying heat? But they were there, dozens of them teeming around the little bamboo dock; and amongst the chocolate natives we couldn't mistake Rick's face, shriveled and sallow, but alive. As our little neoprene raft banged into the pylons, we reached out to make sure he was real. He recounted his ghastly hallucinations, how his toes curled and his skin wrinkled like parchment from dehydration. The vein in the crease of his arm was still black and blue from the massive I.V.s he'd needed in his life-and-death struggle with, not dengue, but typhoid and malaria.

The next day, we gained the east coast of Kalimantan and dined with the missionaries that had seen Rick through. While we marveled at the clockwork of chance that had delivered Rick intact, the missionaries wrote the whole thing off to divine intervention, which sounded marvelous. Borneo was a magical and monstrous land, but we had to get the hell out of there, and fast—to the Tetons, to Glacier National Park, to the North Pole if need be. Somewhere, anywhere that was cold.

Death Valley Sonatas: I & II

By: Paul McHugh

That whole day long, I did just one smart thing. This was to look
out from the crest of the huge curl of wave where I stood, past the
heaved-up shapes of all the other waves, and pick a rough route of
travel that would weave me right past their broad bases. That way, I
wouldn't have to expend the energy required to climb anymore.
And, that way, I might be able to make it back to safety.

The curl of wave I stood upon was almost one hundred feet tall.
It was made of sand.

Safety equated with a 1985 Ford Bronco 4wd truck, one contain-
ing not only a jug of cool water in the back seat but also, up front, a
powerful air conditioner, an automotive climate-control device of
the finest American quality. This Bronco was parked about two
miles off, but a shimmering immensity of hot desert air blurred the
intervening distance. The truck looked an eternity away.

Most likely, that's because I was being cooked to death.

My shoes felt like they were melting into the sand, while my
feet swelled and threatened to burst their laces. The only breaths I
wanted to take were short, shallow, mouse breaths; I didn't dare

9

bring any more searing air deep into my lungs. The big, dry towel that someone had wadded up and crammed into my throat was actually my tongue. My vision and thought were both growing muddled and woozy. Just one thing seemed clear: severe heat stroke was on its way.

I imagined a headline.

"OUTDOOR WRITER KACKS IN DESERT

'Musta been a real greenhorn, getting himself into that sorta fix,' Rangers Say."

One immerses one's self in such troubles slowly at first, and then quickly. That's how it always seems, anyway.

My initial, faint warning of the desert's power came as I ate a tuna fish sandwich in Death Valley, right on a tailgate in the Furnace Creek campground. I opened a fresh loaf of Orowheat Honey Wheatberry bread, spread the tuna salad, laid down the leaf of lettuce. Forty seconds later, when I raised the sandwich to my lips, I was shocked to discover that my bread had already gone stale.

So, we're talking dry. How dry? Try this. Any place that gets less than 10 inches of rain a year can qualify as a desert. Death Valley averages 1.7 inches annually. It's the lowest, hottest, driest stretch of desert in North America.

"We watch dark clouds drift overhead, lots of times," said the national monument's chief ranger, Dick Rayner. "They give forth thunder, rain starts to fall. But it never hits the ground. Giant holes even open up in storms as they cross over here. We see it rain in the mountains all around us, and not a drop reaches us."

At this time, Rayner had spent an even dozen years living here. Seeing a blustery rainstorm show up and try to land a lick on the ground constituted major entertainment.

We're also talking hot. The most incendiary air temperature ever recorded here was 134 degrees Fahrenheit, in July of 1913. But what makes the phenomenon of heat stand out as particularly amazing in the world of Death Valley—which is quite surreal in general—is an aspect called ground temperature.

Certain desert surfaces sop up heat like a sponge, hold and concentrate it, until it soars to a mark 50 percent above air temperature, or even higher. The highest ground temperature ever seen was a whopping 201 degrees, also at the aptly named Furnace Creek, in July of 1972. On that day, the air temperature was just 128.

Those ground surfaces which seem to concentrate and elevate heat the best are salt playa, and—you guessed it—sand dunes.

They (you know, "they") say that the Shoshonean tribe that sparsely inhabited this apparent wasteland called it Tomesha, meaning, "ground on fire." This is a most attractive legend. Unfortunately, like so many exciting legends which seem too good to be true, it may not be. One lonesome authority claims that the real Indian name for the valley was actually Dumbisha, which means "face paint," and refers to the red clay at the mouth of Golden Canyon.

Be that as it may, there's no doubt about how Death Valley got its Euro-American moniker. In 1849, the number of argonauts creaking in wagons across the Great Plains for gold and glory in California swelled to a mighty stream. As winter approached, those bringing up the rear were troubled. The infamous Donner Party, trapped in the snows of the Central Sierra in 1846 and forced into cannibalism to survive, underscored the possibly unappetizing hazards lurking as an unintended consequence of a late start.

Therefore, those wagons leaving the Mormon citadel of Salt Lake City in the inauspicious weeks after September wisely chose a more southerly route. Unwisely, some of them thereafter decided to take a shortcut, following a track sketched in the sand by a Paiute horse thief, and ingenuously recorded in ink and paper by an unduly optimistic onlooker. The onlooker took it to the pioneers, and a lot of them fell for it.

This particular wagon train called itself The San Joaquin Company, though after it hit serious desert the name was aptly corrupted to: The Sand Walking Company. One hundred wagons were organized under the command of a Captain Hunt. Over his protestations, all but two elected to try the horse thief's shortcut. With his brace of wagons of conservatives, Hunt continued on the relatively well-known route to San Bernadino. The others turned directly West, heading straight for a mysterious region that would soon acquire the cognomen of Death Valley.

As they lurched into more and greater difficulties, the majority of the renegades turned south to rejoin Hunt. But lured onward by the snowclad beacon of Telescope Peak, one hundred other individuals pushed on through passes in the Funeral Mountains and next found themselves stumbling across the scorching playas of an amazingly barren valley. This was in the cool of November, but they and their famished oxen were still on their last legs.

What followed was a complex, epic drama of heroism and self-ishness, inspiration and idiocy. In brief and in general, they wound up burning the last of their battered wagons to cure the meat of their oxen, then tried to hike out. They left one human corpse on the valley floor, and twelve more in the mountains to the west. "Goodbye, Death Valley!" one pioneer woman supposedly muttered as she stood in the Panamint Mountains, looking back on the scene of their tribulation.

That name stuck. It was re-validated by subsequent events. A number of get-rich schemers and "single-blanket jackass prospec-tors" descended on Death Valley to uncover the mineral wealth hid-den in the region's rainbows of rock. During the turn-of-the-century mining boom, over 30 people lost their lives by underestimating the stark power of Death Valley's hot and dry.

These included one Jimmy Dayton, a 16-year veteran of the Val-ley, who died while running a six-horse team to the supply center of Dagget. In his final throes, he crawled under the shade of a mesquite bush for a few last seconds of faint succor. The horses, standing by loyally in their traces, also succumbed.

A crusty stage stop operator, Dad Fairbanks, eulogized the legion of departed in this fashion. "Ever' one of 'em just seems to go off his buzz wheel, tears off his shirt, and then commences to diggin'." As if a zone of safety from the hellish sun could be found by going a few inches further away from it, straight down.

Which more or less brings us up to modern times, air-condi-tioned cars and paved highways, polaroid sunglasses, plastic water bottles and canvas hats. Big changes.

But two much bigger things have not really changed out here at all: the power of natural forces, and the folly of human hubris.

On my first trip to Death Valley, I had mostly just driven around, researching the feral burro problem. These escapees from the work-camps of the prospectors, and their prolific progeny, were befouling springs and eating the native desert bighorn sheep out of habitat and home. (These jackasses formed a significant problem for biologists and the government land managers, but this difficulty has since been successfully resolved.)

On my second trip to Death Valley (since I'd already been here one whole time before), I more or less arrived burdened with the notion that I was now a desert expert. Hiking around the Valley on the basis of such a presumption seemed to work out pretty well... at first, anyway.

I trekked into Mosaic and Titus canyons, slid around on the multi-hued clays of the Artists' Palette, examined the weird tracks left by wind-pushed boulders on the broad mud playa of the Devil's Racetrack. Even loaded three gallons of water in a backpack and humped up the long, steep, dry trek to the top of Telescope Peak. I and a girlfriend spent the night up there, first being buffeted by winds rushing out the valley more than two miles below, as an inversion lifted and a mass of super-heated air escaped. Later we admired the tantalizing diamond bracelet of the Milky Way, hanging down through the clear desert sky, a glittering braid that seemed just beyond reach, as we stretched hands out from the warm folds of our sleeping bags.

So hiking into the dunes near Stovepipe Wells figured to be a piece of cake. These sand dunes are a minor yet picturesque presence on Death Valley's sprawling floor. Salt playa, a kind of deep, dry muck with a white, crusty surface, covers 200 square miles of valley bottom. The dunes occupy only 14 square miles. They are graceful, beckoning shapes, seemingly pleasant and innocuous. However, they also are surreal, as if a gigantic beach, levitated from some oceanside resort town, had been arbitrarily dropped here, between desiccated vertebrae of desert mountains.

It's 11 o'clock in the morning, and the air temperature is a tolerable 94 degrees. We are a group of four: myself, my girlfriend, a photographer and his wife. Of us all, I'm the one the most geared-up to go the distance. I'm wearing shorts and hiking shoes, long-sleeved white cotton shirt, sunglasses, daypack with 1.5 quarts of water, and a canvas hat with a cape hanging down in back to shade the neck.

We park the Bronco by the side of the road, and start to walk in. Our goal, our object all sublime, is the highest dune, approximately two miles away. It's a giant, curving monster with a peak reaching between eighty and a hundred feet high, and looks rather like a beige whale breaching amid the frozen waves of all the lesser dunes.

As we leave the highway, we pass through an area crowded with old mesquite bush. As we hike in further, the mesquite grows sparse, its shade becomes less and less, and ground and air temperatures diametrically increase. One by one, my companions drop back and refuse to go further. "We'll just sort of wait here, in the shade," they say. "That'll be fine," I respond. Internally, I say, "Wimps!" My girlfriend is the last to drop off; she says farewell at the fringe of the last mesquite bush.

Feeling muscular, energetic and vital, I plod on into the sand. I'm T. E. Lawrence on the way to Medina, Rommel driving deeper into Egypt. Yes, it's getting real hot, but at least it ain't muggy. Plus, there are no mosquitoes. Once, I busted my hump as a construction laborer all summer in South Florida at the age of 16; if I could take that, I can take anything.

Hmm. Getting real thirsty, all of a sudden. Well, that's what the water bottle is for, by God, and I'm carrying much more than I could ever hope to need. So, I unscrew the top and guzzle, guzzle, then splash some of the extra onto my shirt and hat. As this evaporates, I become my own swamp cooler. Deucedly clever, what?

Onward!

Hmm. It's getting a little confusing down here in the gullies between the dunes. These things writhe every which-a-way. What's the best direction to take toward that big sucker? Better climb a small one, and see.

Hmm. Man, traction really sucks on this steep sand. You take a step, slip halfway back. Take a step, slip halfway back. Even on the level, your normal push-off doesn't net anywhere near as much gain as it could on firmer soil. So we've got to mentally chop the pace to a tall granny gear. Compound low. Be patient.

This is simply going to take more time than you reckoned.

Hmm. OK, there's that big dude dune I'm gonna claim, but it still looks as far away as it ever did. Must be some trick of distortion in the air.

Now, I'm thirsty again. Well, drink! But this tepid water swills right down my throat and vanishes to no effect, like I'm drinking nothing. And now the bottle's more than half gone. How did that happen?

As I plod onward, I realize that my skin is starting to feel like parchment, and that the reason I don't seem to be sweating is not because I'm NOT sweating, but because the scorching air reaches right down into my pores and evaporates my fluids before they even reach the surface.

I feel a tad light-headed, and a thought scurries across my mind: maybe to insist on bagging that big dune might not be such a great idea. I pause, turn, and look back at the line of mesquite bushes. I'm now at a point equidistant between the shade and the peak. A dry Rubicon.

Ah, don't be a wimp, I tell myself. A modicum of impeccable will, a dash of Nietzsche, a bit of Carlos Casteneda, a little Norman Vincent Peale, that's all that's required, here. Let's think positive. You'll make it. You've just gotta WANT it enough.

Onward. Finally, at the base of the big dune, it's decision-time again. I gulp the last pitiful sip of grit-laden water from the bottom of my water bottle. I'm aware of feeling woozy and weak. And I've noted that deep inside these dunes, I've discovered pockets of heat way more intense than anything I'd ever experienced before. For safety's sake, I should probably just drop my plan to bag that big one.

But... this is my last day in Death Valley. And I've made it this far. And I really want to see the view from the top. Maybe all that's really required is a rallying of will and a summoning of the spirit. Mind over matter, don't you know. Most important of all: it would be kind of embarrassing to come back to my friends and have to say, hey I was almost there. But ultimately, you know, I lacked the genuine moxie to make it.

So. Onward and upward. Hey, the windward side of this dune is really steep. Take a two-foot step, and you'll slide back down until your net gain is only about four inches. I feel like Sisyphus up here. It's a goldang sand treadmill. And I don't really have time to screw around! I've got to get up and off this thing and out of here! A small gust of panic drifts through my mind, like a ragged red caul carried on a puff of disjointed thought.

That is followed by a ray of hope, when I make it up onto the spine of the big dune, and find myself plodding on toward the summit. I am Ahab hauling himself on harpoon ropes up along the spine of a beige Moby... in that archetype of all Pyrrhic victories.

Finally, I reach the peak. I would raise my arms and exult, but my mouth seems plugged with cotton batting, and I have not an erg of spare energy for any Rocky-style macho displays. The view from atop the big dune is, in fact, stunning. But I now perceive I could wind up being rather permanently stunned by it.

I feel exhausted, weak and ill. Perhaps an early sign that my petty triumph on the peak of this sand lump could wind up as a net debit. That's when I do my single smart thing, and gaze out across this broad jumble of dunes, trying to extract some idea of their hidden order, so that I can devise a short, efficient route of return to safety. Next, I follow this micro-second of brilliance with an act that is supremely dumb.

In high school physics, I'd studied the principle of the parabola. We all did. We know how parabolic curves can focus waves of light, sound, or radio, and why parabolas are used to shape everything from a satellite dish to a microscope lens. In fact, right on the west rim of Death Valley, I'd had a recent refresher course at the Charcoal Kilns. These were built of native rock in the late 1800's to help miners cook up pinyon charcoal for smelting ore. The ten kilns, 25 feet high, were designed to focus fiery heat in an anaerobic environment.

Now that they've been empty for a century or so, you find upon entering that they can concentrate sound waves in the same efficient fashion. Stand within, at a focal point of their compound parabolic curves, and you'll be bathed in perfect resonance as you sing or speak. Just like you were some cardinal warbling on a throne in a cathedral of your personal Holy See.

But, regrettably, I didn't key in this information while hiking toward the tallest dune. I'd been aware that the blasts of heat through which I wandered seemed to undulate in scale. But I did not figure out that it was the very shape and curves of the dunes, themselves, that could concentrate or relieve the degree of intensity.

My big, dumb move now is to take the short, fast route off the tall dune. I jump, and run straight down the slipface. Now the slipface of a dune is on its steep lee side, where the windblown grains rest at their highest angle of repose (34 degrees). This face, from top to bottom and from side to side, is fashioned by wind into one huge set of compound curves.

It's a sand parabola. A lens.

I have just about a single second to congratulate myself on figuring out the right sort of galloping, leaping stride to use in the loose sand as I run. Then I suddenly find myself plunging through a hot zone that sears the inside of my nostrils, and makes my lungs clench involuntarily.

It's as though a pool of lighter fluid has collected in the family barbecue, and it explodes in my face as I toss in a match. I can practically hear my hair frizz and crinkle, feel my skin shrivel. I wind up stumbling in shock, falling, skidding down to the bottom of the dune on my hands and knees.

Great. Now I'm in the classic posture of all those desert explorers in the cartoons, crawling on hands and ragged knees toward the odalisque... who holds an icy water pitcher, and beckons me to crawl further into the mirage.

My position may be ludicrous, but it is not funny.

How hot is it? During the hour I was out in the dunes, the air temperature rose to 104 degrees. Taking the 30 to 50 percent increase of ground temperature possible, and pegging it at the high end because of the focusing power of the dune, I had probably just stumbled through a zone of 150 to 160 degrees Fahrenheit.

My remaining energy is now sapped. The only thing left to do is tap the dregs. I struggle to my feet, and step forward. My legs are leaden. Two miles to tramp back to safety. Seems impossible. I hold just one image uppermost in my mind: the pattern of gullies and waves in the dunes that I'd glimpsed from the top, and a hypothetical route through them that I must follow if I'm to ever make it out of here.

One of old Sam Johnson's most lasting contributions to literature is probably his bit that goes, "When a man knows he's to be hanged in a fortnight, it concentrates his mind wonderfully."

Believe me, at this point, I'd love to concentrate my mind. But my brain no longer seems to work very well. Amid this baking heat, my head feels like a tea-kettle on a stove burner. I can almost hear the internal, whistling sound of a plummeting IQ level as steam comes billowing out my ears.

Push has, in fact, come to shove.

The basics of heat stroke are these. The body's normal internal temperature is, of course, the famous 98.6. The temperature of the skin is normally 92 degrees Fahrenheit. Any excess internal heat is carried to the surface of the skin, where it is dissipated. However, if the external AIR temperature grows hotter than 92 degrees, this becomes progressively more difficult.

The body has two methods of enhancing the heat transfer and dissipation. One is to dilate or widen the capillaries or small veins on the surface of the skin, which increases the flow of hot blood from internal organs and radiates the heat away. The other method is perspiration, which cools the skin through process of evaporation, with heat agitating the water molecules until they waft off as vapor.

During episodes of prolonged, extreme heat, both these methods can easily grow overtaxed. Resting quietly in the shade on a 110-degree day, your average human will lose about a quart of water per hour through perspiration, in the body's effort to stay cool. When exercising heavily in direct sunlight, in temperatures above 120 degrees, even a gallon of water per hour may not be enough. The water may not make it through your gut fast enough to reach the surface of your skin.

Then the water in your flesh will be sucked out faster than you can replace it. One gallon of water weighs eight pounds. If you lose five percent of your body weight in moisture, you will experience feelings of nausea. Lose six to ten percent, and you experience dizziness, difficulty breathing, and weakness from the sluggish movement of thickened blood.

Lose fifteen to twenty percent, and you've just joined Jimmy Dayton and the unlucky members of The Sand Walking Company on a direct shortcut to the Hereafter.

As perspiration wicks off, dries up, and fails, your body may make one last mighty effort to dissipate heat through extreme dilation of capillaries. But as your internal temperature rises five, six, seven, eight degrees, life becomes impossible. At 112 degrees, the very protein that holds you together starts to break down.

The precious pink jelly of brain tissue becomes critically stressed as the big arteries in the neck carry your superheated blood upwards; then consciousness goes nova in a final frenzy of dementia. This is heat stroke.

You fly off your buzzwheel, as Dad Fairbanks so cogently and ungently put it.

I do not, at the time of my risky trek through the dunes, understand these changes intellectually. However, viscerally, I come to grasp them quite well.

No matter how hard I try to hold it before me and follow its beckoning, my map of the route I must follow wavers, slips and flips in my mind like a funhouse mirror. I'm not sure that I can even hold to one steady direction. I may just be staggering around in circles.

Way off in the distance now, I can hear a faint call. It's not a desert raven, mocking me with raucous laughter... although maybe that's what it should be. It's my friends, calling out my name. I want to answer, but I assess my energy, and find that I cannot. To utter a shout would take a moist throat, and all the energy required to move one or two steps, and I cannot risk losing any steps. All movement forward is very important, very tough, and requires my full concentration.

But I am touched by their concern. Even though it feels quite faint and distant, I suck vital energy from their caring like a psychic vampire. My girlfriend is a very good kisser. If I were to croak out here, I think, I would kind of miss that... and so I take two more steps forward. Three.

And they've really done me a bigger service than they know. If their voices are still coming from off to my left, then I still must be moving roughly toward the road. I'm not stumbling in circles. It's amazing how grateful I feel for this crumb of reinforcement that is drifting in my direction.

I find that I vaguely envy them for their good sense in staying in the shade. It's interesting to consider just how swiftly and completely I've been transformed from a cocky outdoorsman into a shambling, demented beggar. Desert mojo is strong medicine.

At the fringe of mesquite bush, my urge to lie down in the scant shade nearly overwhelms every other thought or impulse.

Just think, I could just sort of rest here for a while, and I would no longer be broiling myself alive. I'd only be cozy and snug, like a pup curled up in sunbeams on a soft, fluffy rug. Then my friends or the rangers would later find me, and coo over me, and bring me Coca-Colas to drink and cool cloths for my brow, and I'd be just fine.

And that would be infinitely more pleasant than having to raise these fat, heavy legs of mine, each one weighing well over three hundred pounds. In fact, that's probably where all of my water went, it ran down into my legs. If I could just get horizontal for a comfy second or two in the shade, then some of it might run back up to my parched throat. ...

Hey, yeah, that's the ticket! Lie down, and get the water moving up from my shoes!

A dim corner of my consciousness realizes that the rest of my mind is starting to sound pretty goddam batso. This corner of sanity heroically leaps up, walls the rest of my mind off like the cosmonaut pulling plugs on HAL in *2001*, then locks itself into my control room and hot-wires the intercom to all my torpid musculature.

"Keep moving, asshole!" it barks.

OK. Yessir. I regret that I have only one nap to surrender for my country. Into the valley of death rode the gallant one... one... one... one step at a time, big fella. That's all it takes. Die with your boots on. That's the only way they're ever gonna let you wear that Marshall's badge.

Not to mention the brittlebush cluster with the salt sprinkles...

And then I'm through the mesquite and at the edge of the road
There's the Bronco, parked about 150 yards away. Keys are still in
my pocket, good. I hobble up to the door. Oh no. I can no longer
recognize the right key. I fumble, drop them. Woozily pick them up,
try about five. The door opens. Get in, start engine, turn on air conditioner, and all but stuff myself through the vents trying to get my
whole body into the heart of that supreme, delicious coolness as it
fans out toward me.

Catch a glimpse of myself in the rearview mirror, and I am thor-
oughly startled: I look like a demon. All my skin, even the white of
my eyes, has turned a fiery, brick red, from my capillaries' last-
ditch attempt to dissipate heat.

I still cannot speak, but I honk the Bronco's horn with one hand
in order to let my friends know that I'm back and alive. As I turn to
snatch the water jug up from the rear seat, I see them run up to the
car, their faces wearing expressions that mingle concern and relief.

"Hey, we were really starting to get worried about you," my girlfriend says.

"Blrkgpt... ack!" I explain.

Then I close my eyes and pour sweet cool water into my mouth
while stars of pleasure wheel and explode in my brain.

II.

And so I wised up.

The next time I hiked into the Death Valley sand dunes, I was
much better prepared: I went without a hat, shirt or sunglasses, and
carried only about half the water I'd taken previously.

I also went about ten o'clock at night, with a full moon riding
high and benign in a blueblack desert sky. The air was a sultry 80
degrees, and gradually growing cooler, not hotter. It was about eight
years after the episode of my great internal infernal cookery, and I
was no longer out here trying to prove anything to anyone.

I was simply here to enjoy myself.

I parked a Subaru Brat in about the same spot where a Bronco
had once been, and hiked in on approximately the same route.
Those things were the same, but the dunes had shifted remarkably

from the way they'd been during my previous excursion, eight years ago. Sand waves may not be quite as fluid as ocean swells, but probably shift along similar lines and principles.

Instead of one large dune, now there were three big ones out there, shimmering high above all the others in the moonshine. I took a sighting between Tucki Mountain on the southwest valley rim and Corkscrew Peak on the northeast rim, so that I'd have an accurate bearing to travel on, even when walking down in the gulches.

As I left the line of creosote bush, I noted how the plates of mud playa turned their edges up in astonishment at the gradually increasing impact of ambient sand. Then the mud disappeared, and it was all sand underfoot. Again, I felt forward thrust of each step diminish, and adjusted my pace accordingly.

But, as the Kiwis say, I had no worries, mate.

In the cool of night, there was time and mind to consider the swirl and heft of change that continually raised, then razed, this palimpsest of sand upon which I trod.

Death Valley is a fault basin, a "graben," rather than a true valley. That means instead of being scooped out by a glacier or river erosion, the bottom fell out of it through massive earthquakes and geologic plate shifts along fault lines. These epic shudders and displacements also raised mountain ranges up on each side while the bottom dropped. Essentially, then, the real valley floor is a long way down. It's estimated the bedrock of it is located under layers of sediment and erosion fans about 8,000 feet thick. This sediment is the sloughed-off remnants of all the previous surrounding mountains.

If that was removed, the vertical relief from the top of Telescope Peak to the lowest point in the valley would total 19,049 feet, exceeding that of McKinley's north slope, and making it the highest relief on the continent.

Anyway, all that geologic activity around the gigantic mud sump of the valley floor reared up big mountains striped with the limestone and coral of ancient seas, black lava flows, pink muds, compacted sediments, low grade marble, quartz, gneiss and "fanglomerate"—old alluvial deposits hardened into ersatz rock. In bursts of The Cosmic Potter's playfulness, these strata got folded, broken, and tipped up on end.

Now, these peaks are being gradually hammered into fragments by blasts of stark sunlight, by wind, rain and frost, and scraped down ever so slightly by the scurrying claws of peripatetic chuck-wallas. In this fashion, the mountains surrender mineral crystals that become "blow sand," the very finest in spare mountain parts.

Amid winds of ten miles per hour or more, this sand begins to blow across the landscape, seldom getting more than six feet off the ground. The smaller grains fly, the heavier grains hop and creep in a movement that soil scientists call "saltation."

These mineral grains wander like tumbleweeds until the more obdurate aspects of the landscape—like Tucki Mountain—or cross-winds tumbling in from another canyon, cause prevailing winds to spin, eddy, then slow and drop their burden. And so, dunes start to build. And the wind does not cease work, but continues to rake and comb its creation into hills that shapeshift and migrate. It would be fascinating to possess time-lapse photos that could swiftly show the dune movements of a century or more. Such images linked in a fast film clip would surely resemble a pod of beige whales, plunging slowly through huge, turbid seas.

I approach the tallest dune of the three, pausing to wave a mosquito away from my ear. So, mosquitoes do come out here! At night, anyway. Surely, these errant insects are the very Magellens, the absolute Vasco da Gamas of the bug world. They must've been flying all the way from the creeks in Cottonwood Canyon, easily 12 miles away. How brave of them to dare the dry dunes in search of mammalian blood. I wonder if any would ever be able to find their way back to water to lay their brood.

Up onto the spine of the big one, and then along to the peak. I grow slightly impressed with myself. How had I summoned the grit and folly to climb this slippery thing in harsh heat of mid-day? The diminishment of mental power must've come on earlier than I'd suspected.

Sitting on the top, now. No wind stirs. There were crickets in the creosote, but out here in the broad billows of sand, the desert rings with stillness.

I drag fingertips in the sand, plowing a small mimicry of the end-less intricate furrows I see, traced in the dune surfaces by wind.

I note that the delicate tracery of these lines, on the dune's windward face at least, is aligned with the wind's path. But on the slipface, the lines shift direction, become perpendicular to prevailing winds, back here where tumbling gusts, stubbing their toes on the crest, rotate and drop their burden.

How odd such an erratic thing as swirls and currents of wind can create patterns in the sand that seem so regular, yet random. So random, yet regular.

Then, I get my big Aha! experience.

My gaze shifts up and outward and I see that this same regular, random pattern is recognizable in the overall placement of the big dunes, as well. A shiver goes down my spine, as I behold this.

It was a perception of that pattern, and a holding of its map in my mind, which had saved my goose from being completely cooked, eight years ago. Now, with a cool patience that I can fully afford, even though the pattern is bathed only in dim silver of moonlight, I see it more clearly than before.

And I gaze out past the dunes into ghost mountains wrought of time, moonlight, mass and shadow, and see more than physical distance. I imagine the scrape and jingle of the pioneer wagons, the weak bawling of tormented oxen. My perspective also encompasses the gulf between Stupid and Smart, between Survival and Slaughter. Writers, adventurers, outdoorsmen, all human beings perhaps, like to emphasize the moments of high danger, when everything seems to hang in the balance. But dulcet moments such as this one now, when decent decisions have been made, all circumstance is calm and ordered, and comprehension seems the same size as the world.... Such moments can be as gripping as crisis, yet satisfy one more, as they affirm the sweetness possible in life.

Almost midnight. Time to go.

This moment must be marked.

Instead of rising to my feet, I flip over backwards off the crest and joyously perform somersaults, rolling over and over as I tumble down the slipface of the big dune. The moon and stars rotate crazily in my peripheral vision. Sand jams itself in my hair and ears and pockets and shoes. But I don't care. This is fun!

Laughing, I stagger to my feet, and set my course southwest, on a line between Corkscrew and Tucki mountains. I remind myself that I'm not the only entity to move around at night. Kangaroo rats emerge from their narrow burrows under the mesquite and creosote bushes, to gambol and gather their seeds. The sidewinders also come out, seeking to rendezvous with the rats, as they loop across the sand.

And so if you hike at night, you have to look out for the sidewinders.

It is, after all, the desert.

Sanders, '93

Hanging by My Lips

By: Michael Hodgson

I enjoy climbing, really I do. It's just that I do not subscribe to all the genre magazines of the pumped and beautiful, nor do I practice fingernail pull-ups so that if the need ever arose, I could hang 600 ft. off the ground by only my index finger. Believe me, if the need ever really arose, and it would not be by choice, I could hang 600 ft. off the ground by my nose hair and I sure as hell wouldn't need any practice runs.

OK, I admit it, I am building a climbing wall in my garage, but only because it will help me dream of greatness, of being there. Nothing like a few laps up and down a wall to really help one relive the moment after reading books like *Half Dome Without Ropes and Blindfolded*. Actually, if you were to classify me as a climber, I would rate right up there with the born-to-be-sandbagged and the truly average.

All my buff climbing friends know this, my wife knows this, even my dog probably knows this, but do I ever remember it at critical moments like when my "friends" say, "let's go climbing dude." Nahhhh. In those brief seconds between invitation and decision, my cerebral thought process ceases, causing all rational concepts to short circuit and fantasy to take over. I am man, I am invincible. Besides, we are only climbing an easy route they say. Right, and I'm the King of Persia.

One such incident (one of many over the years if truth be known) occurred a while back in Joshua Tree National Monument, California—the winter climbing Mecca and most holy of destinations for climbers the world over.

Bob, a good friend and expert climber, had enthusiastically invited me to go climbing with him at the last minute (he probably couldn't find anyone else), offering to teach me the nuances of multi-pitched climbs and, if I did well enough, to actually let me lead a climb or two. Bob must have really been desperate.

I studied the climbs Bob had mapped out for us. They didn't seem too bad, on paper. It's rather difficult to translate one-dimensional descriptions into three dimensional vertical fear-factor routes of immense proportions. This might actually be fun!

"By the way, there's one climb I thought of this morning, just before we left," Bob casually commented. "It's not in the book you have there, but it's a great warm-up route. I thought we'd shoot up that one first, just for starters. I think it's rated 5.6 or something like that—couple of tough moves, but nothing you can't handle."

I remembered thinking no problem although wondering why Bob was being vague on the rating. Still, 5.6 was easily within my established ability and if Bob thought it was a good warm-up, then it must be so.

Bob flashed the route, pausing only briefly to dust his hands once or twice in climber's chalk. He's up and grinning. "Piece of cake, you're going to love this one." Never trust a friend who can tie knots with one hand, climb with the other and always shows up to climb in shoes that look like ballet slippers and tights that are color coordinated with both his T-shirt and truck. One of these days, I'll take my own advice.

The morning started off well enough, a few quick, artistic moves and I was disentangled from the seat belt and clipped into a rope at the base of the rock face. At this point, the climb began to increase in difficulty, chiefly because from base on, it was all up.

Grunting and wheezing I grabbed at hand holds that, on the ground would seem huge, but as I groped even higher seemed to grow incrementally smaller, almost minuscule. After sixty feet of scuffing, huffing and puffing—all because I was being forced to remove the nine million bits of protection (that's Friends, Nuts, and Chocks you idiots, not rubbers!) Bob had placed as practice for me—I found myself staring at an overhang. An overhang for gosh sakes! I didn't know they made overhangs on 5.6 rated climbs.

Bravely, and because I still blindly trusted the minute particle of my brain that insisted if Bob said this was a 5.6 climb it was a 5.6 and nothing more, I inched my way up under the overhang and then, oh god, reached out and around into space. I fumbled and scratched for anything that seemed as if it would provide a gripping surface for my increasingly sweaty fingers—nothing. As I clawed and scraped for a hold, the thought occurred to me that Bob had sort of casually mentioned that his belay anchor wasn't all that solid. Did he mean "not all that solid" as in if I fell I was going to fall a long way? Or "not all that solid" as in, old anchors and webbing but nothing really to worry about with a top rope situation. Nothing like uncertainty with the anchor and your belay man to inch up the pucker factor.

Bob yelled, "There's nothing to hold onto there, you'll have to use the crack. Just jam your hands and toes in and work your way out and up—the jams are bomber dude!"

Jam my way? Jamming is what rock groups and other musicians do. I had come to climb—you know, up a face on nice, easy-to-grab features that provided a modicum of excitement without fear of death or dismemberment. Instead, Bob was yelling at me to jam?

I had read somewhere that you place your fist, fingers and/or toes sideways into a crack, twist them until they grabbed at the rock, or vice versa. Then, carefully and successively weight your hands and feet and up you go. Sounded easy enough—Hah! Tentatively, I placed one hand and twisted it into place. Then the other. Hey, look Ma, no hands! I was jammin'! Twisting my toes into place and then placing one hand/one foot after another, I worked my way, inch by inch, out and around the overhang. This technique was working wonderfully until, holy shit! The crack began getting wider than my hands and I began slipping towards my doom.

Forget technique and proper hand/foot placement—I opted for partial body jams. Using my elbows, knees, shoulders, head, anything I could stuff into the crack except my manhood (I was saving that for a real emergency) I struggled and swore my way up and past the overhang and back onto the joy of a vertical rock wall with nothing above me but blue sky and Bob's smiling face—fifty feet away.

Clinging to the rock at what now seemed to be a bazillion feet above the earth's surface, on a virtually smooth, featureless sandstone cliff-face that even an ant wouldn't be caught dead on, my senses returned with a blinding fury, opening the door for Fear.

This, in turn, sent vibrations through my legs causing them to shake and hop rather like an old Singer sewing machine. Although I had planned on staying put until Bob figured out a way to haul me up, my new found vibration technique began moving me along the tiny ledge, without any assistance or forethought from me.

As it was, the ledge began to grow incrementally smaller, disappearing into a narrow dihedral crack—the crux of the climb. Believe me, I didn't plan on traversing this, but my vibrating body had other ideas. It was shake, rattle and roll all the way across and up fifteen feet of ledge and crack. Michael Jackson? Forget it. He can moonwalk on a stage for sure, but I was moonwalking, crack walking, shimmying and tapping my way sixty feet above the earth.

"Nice moves!" my "friend" screamed hysterically, tears running down his face.

Meanwhile, quite a crowd had gathered below, obviously amazed at the skill required to dance on such a tiny ledge and quite possibly wondering why there had been no advance billing for such an incredible act.

I am not sure what possesses me when all looks hopeless and out of hand, but somehow I always seem to manage an extraordinary surge of effort that pulls my life out of the ever tightening grip of disaster. Perhaps I was inspired by the fact that all those craning necks below were beginning to look deathly far away, or maybe it was a feeling that if I didn't reach the top, I would be wimping out on a measly 5.6 climb that I used to be able to cruise up—I have yet to accept the aging process gracefully. Whatever the motivation, I do know that by using knee squeezes, lip jams, butt stuffs, pelvic thrusts, full body hugs, and incredible sphincter control, I managed to squirm and snarl my way up the remaining fifty feet to terra firma and flat, horizontal terrain.

Respectful applause could be heard below, probably because after one hour, everyone was getting very impatient to climb and also because they were very grateful that I hadn't fallen on them. Bob clapped me enthusiastically on the back and gushed "Gosh, I almost can't believe how easily you made it up that 5.10. I thought you said you could only climb 5.6."

I probably should have said something to him, thanked him for the encouragement and support, or hit him with a fusillade of obscenity, but I was too busy remembering how to tie a hangman's knot—Bob deserved to die.

Tirado los Tubos

By: John Long

I had packed up and headed back to Venezuela. Solomon's Army couldn't handle the work I had a month to finish, but I went anyway. Mariana planned to flee her teaching job in the phoneless jungle for a week to visit friends and family in El Tigre, her home town. If I didn't join her, brother Luis Manuel would pistol whip me on my next visit.

I hooked up with Mariana in Maracaibo, and also Jimmy, her cousin. Jimmy and I had attended college together in the states, and during spring break of our senior year I'd gone down to Venezuela with him, and had met Mariana. Jimmy had a master's degree in computer science and some fancy government job, but his greater capacity was for knavery and plenty of it. A sworn coward, he nonetheless seemed always to find himself in the middle of impossible adventures and intrigues—with governor's wives; with the truculent Yajiros, the local Indians; on jungle canoe trips that always got lost, once for forty-six days. Jimmy Cepeda was God's original fool, and the best friend I ever had.

We piled into Jimmy's van and after a marathon drive, finally wheeled into El Tigre, a blistering savannah peppered with mint thickets, mapora palms and galloping oil rigs. Many "Yanqui" engineers hole up here in vast, hermetically sealed campamientos from which they never leave save to the airport. The mercury sizzled at ninety-seven in the shade, if you could find any.

The cement house went wild when we arrived. Three-hundred pound Grandmama stopped kneading the arepa and quavered to her feet. Niece Pepina, six-foot one and thin as a caco quill, dashed over with a tray of pigs feet al carbon as a dozen kids sprung from shady nooks. A Latin home is rarely in want of kids, because the people pride themselves on getting married when they want, not when they should; and they're quick to fashion a couple niños because they can. Three years before, I'd been the first gringo to ever enter their house, or their neighborhood, but so long as I was Jimmy's friend—and now Mariana's fiancee—the house, and everything in it, was mine.

Brother Luis Manuel suddenly rushed in, ten-gallon hat perched just above his dark eyes and foot-long pistola in his hand. A thick, mustachioed thirty-five year old with the face of a hangman, he worked sixty-hour-a-week shifts at the petro-chemical plant outside El Tigrito to maintain the dignity of the house. He rushed past Jimmy and I into the jardin to fire three glorious rounds into the sky. Then he laid down a few creole dance steps, booted a sleeping dog, cracked his bullwhip, fired a fourth shot into a stump, and slapped my back till I gasped. His black eyes needled down:

"Matrimonio? Cuando?"

When I mentioned a very tentative date for the wedding, Luis Manuel's eyes fired like cannons. He kissed Mariana, then me, then Pepina, then Jimmy, then Grandmama, then he broke back into his dancing, faster this time. He made for his pistol but was halted by a bottle of Cacique proffered in Grandmama's plump and stingy hand. He'd swilled four fingers before Pepina snatched it back for Grandmama to lock in a chipped wooden cabinet to which there was only one key—the silver skeleton Grandmama tucked back into her black lace brassiere, a fallow acre no man sober or drunk would dare trespass.

We all sat down and feasted through kilos of bisteak, fried plantains, ensalada aguacate, crunchy sheets of casabe, quarts of jugo de tamarindo and various colorful sweet tubers whose names I could never get my tongue around; and I slowly reentered the emphatic world of a culture which, candid and open as the savannah, lived like everybody would if they could stop worrying about life and start living it.

Later, Grandmama got a headache. That prompted a trip to the pharmacia for headache medication, an expedition of exactly three blocks. Luis Manuel could have walked there and back in six minutes, but he'd take the pickup—because he had one, because it had a full tank, because he'd washed and waxed it earlier that day, and because it had straight-pipes and when he gunned it, which he normally did, it sounded like Krakatoa erupting in spurts. And all this made the man seem more magnificent as he thundered down the street to the cheers and jeers of friends lounging in thresholds and in hammocks on their verandas. Luis would not travel alone, because going to the pharmacia in the pickup was an event, and an event in Venezuela, no matter how big or how small, is always performed in numbers.

I wedged myself into the bed of the pickup among thirteen kids, four dogs and Grandmama, who Luis Manuel, Jimmy and I had conveyed there in an easy chair, and who would check the date on the medication to ensure it was bueno. As Luis gunned the truck down the road, the frame sagging to the pavement, the great straight-pipes blasted three-foot flames as whoops roared from every house we passed.

Back in the house, as I watched a red gekko creep across a peeling whitewashed wall, Luis Manuel laid out his plan. Or started to.

"Ave Maria Purisima! What now?" Jimmy laughed. Later, he would explain to me about Luis' "plans," epics that always had him fearing for his life, but which he could never refuse. Most memorable had been bulldogging range donkeys, a stunt that cost Luis Manuel several teeth and a fractured collarbone.

"Tirado los tubos!" Luis said.

"Shooting the tubes?" Jimmy asked.

"Si, chamo," said Luis Manuel. Then he explained.

During construction of the nearly completed hydro-electric plant in Tascabana, thirty miles out of town, the Carina Indians had discovered tube-shooting through accident. The plant's cooling system required rerouting all the surrounding rivers; this was accomplished with three-foot diameter steel tubes that piped water along a twisting route to a central aqueduct. "Tirada los tubos" was to intentionally do what had accidentally happened to a young Indian boy who, while diving for crayfish, got drawn into one of the half-filled drainage tubes. He became a human torpedo, speeding in black, downhill passage for hundreds of yards before his free-fall exit into the deep aqueduct.

So we could get a clear picture, Luis Manuel assumed various dive-bomb positions on the cement floor until he spotted a terrific cucaracha on yonder wall—a three-incher, black as sin. He sprang for his bullwhip, but Pepina thrust her pool-cue leg out and tripped him. The roach zipped into a chink in the wall beyond the lunging boys, and the roof nearly blew off for all the laughing, particularly that of Grandmama, who then farted like a tent ripping. Again, she howled so hard the key to the liquor cabinet clinked from her dress. Luis Manuel dove for it, but got only a handful of Pepina's moccasin. Grandmama repositioned the key back in no-man's land, then broke wind again, and we all just had to clear the hell out.

Luis Manuel fanned himself with his hat, and spit for effect, grieving that the next day would mark the end of tube shooting. They were to weld grates over the tube's entrances when the plant fired up on Monday. The chickens were roosting. The dog had fled to Ecuador. And we were out of beer. Luis Manuel grabbed his bullwhip to look for cockroaches.

We headed out for Tascabana and the tubes early the next morning, rumbling through a scattering of drowsy pueblos. On the outskirts of Rocas Negras, population 56, I noted an adobe shack topped by a peeling icon gaudy as a circus bill and exactly three times as tall as the shack. The icon featured a ravaged Jesus dragging the cross toward Golgatha. Several soldiers were whipping our Savoir, who, under a crown of thorns the size of a tractor tire, stumbled on, drenched in blood. A perpetual queue of people, mainly children and old women half in mourning, were filing in one side of the shack and out another. One hundred heaps were parked along the road.

"For fifty Boliveras, you can get in line to see part of Jesus' genuine crown of thorns," Jimmy said.

"Really," I said, craning my neck to study the grisly icon.

"But it's only a small part," Jimmy added, as Luis Manuel swerved past a woman with a shawl pulled over her head.

"In Caracas, they got a whole one."

"Verrrrrga!!" Jimmy yelled as Luis Manuel wheeled his pickup toward the sprawling mob at Tascabana. I figured there were easily 2,000 people already there. Some had driven from as far away as Ciudad Bolivar. Others had punished their burros upwards of two days across torrid plains to shoot the tubes, or drink, or both. The City Council and the National Guard had drummed up various safety procedures—all needless—and a phalanx of soldiers was there to enforce them.

From atop two junkers parked on opposite banks of an Olympic-sized mudhole, the Mayor of Tascabana (Don Armando Brito, renown for having read nothing except funny papers and the Bible) and one Coronel Baltazar Negretti de Negron megaphoned commands, which sounded like so much white noise, challenged as they were by the distorted stereos of five-hundred cars that girded the sump in a formation so tight that Luis Manuel, Jimmy and I had to tread over trunks, roofs and hoods just to gain the tubes. At the waterline, entrepreneurs peddled deep-fried pig skin and bottled pop, and already the lagoon was awash in trash equaling that of a World Cup soccer match. Enriched by the harshest liquors, hundreds laughed, jeered and shouted, anxious to go before their valor washed downstream. Bobbing pop cans, plastic wrappers, soccer balls, a guitar, two stray dogs and dozens of humans rapidly drained down the twenty-odd tubes, continuously replaced by roof hoppers on the rebound, bruised and horror-stricken, but ready for more. However, Luis Manuel seemed suspicious of the thick layer of foam in the water and would have nothing of this common man's launch.

"He wants to go to the higher pool," Jimmy moaned. "Faster tubes up there."

"Lead the way," I said. Jimmy looked like a convict marching to the gallows, yet seemed dead-set on getting hanged.

Our bare feet made rude slurping sounds in the mud as we followed Luis Manuel a quarter mile to the higher pool. This one had a tenth the people, half the tubes, and five times the soldiers. I waded in and stroked for a tube, but—Alto! A soldier would first have to take an "official" ride.

"Por que?!" begged Luis Manuel.

"El gordo, el gordisimo!" laughed a private, knee-deep in the murky water and clutching a rifle that predated de Miranda's landing at Corto. It seemed some fatty had just taken off, so the scout would have to go first—to flush the tube.

Luis Manuel grabbed our arms and the three of us stroked over to another tube and slipped in—me clutching Luis Manuel's ankles, Jimmy, sheet-white and trembling, clinging onto mine. The turns were five-degree welded elbows, so at turn one, the three of us were jolted apart, as were half of Luis Manuel's remaining teeth and most of my vertebrae. Due to the constant water flow, the tubes were well mossed, and in seconds we were vaulting down into blackness. Bam! We slammed through another turn. "If I hit another bend, I'll dent the fucking tube," I thought, trying to ignore the screams of careening bodies echoing about. After a long minute and hundreds of yards, just as my stomach had shrunk to the size of a chickpea, light showed far ahead. Then, POP! We rifled out and free fell into casual water, flailing to avoid hitting each other. We swam to shore and started rubbing our barked hips and shoulders. Nobody could stop laughing and Jimmy carried on as though he'd just slayed the Hydra with his bare hands.

"It takes a set of bollas to take that ride, chico!" he yelled. "Bolla grandes!"

We kicked back in the mud, and watched for a while. I noticed that better than half of the tube-shooters were women and girls, but Jimmy kept on about his "bolla grandes."

A fifty-foot cement wall was festooned with more than forty pissing tubes, whose positions varied from below the waterline to fifty-feet above it. From the profusion of tubes, I felt assured of Luis Manuel's claim that all pipes terminated here, allaying Jimmy's fear that some strange pipe might spit us out in Paraguay. Screaming bodies came whistling forth, backward, upside down landing on friends who had landed on friends. Everyone howled watching them, stunned and dumfounded, hobble over to the bank, collapse into the mud and lick their wounds.

"Coooooono!" shrieked Luis Manuel.

I just caught sight of a crazed youth who came rocketing out at the fifty-foot level. His scream could have frozen a fifth of Ron Oro, and his arms pawed the air like an airborne cat as everyone below dove for their lives. WHOP! A ten-point belly flop. Yet he quickly stroked to the bank and raced off.

"Vamo, pue!" Luis Manuel said, jumping up.

"The bastard can't let that kid out do us," Jimmy said to me, white and shaking again.

We scampered after the kid, but lost him in the crowd. Plodding on, I noticed steady traffic staggering to and from a cordoned area surrounded by a dozen menacing soldiers.

"Oh, that?" Jimmy said, relieved that we'd lost the kid. "Liquor is strictly forbidden anywhere near the tubes. Too dangerous. But anyone willing to walk to that huddle can drink himself half dead and go right back to the pipes. You figure it out."

Back at the high mudhole, Luis Manuel spotted some footprints leading off, and the three of us tracked them half a mile to a green puddle, vacant save for the kid we'd just seen delivered fifty feet above the aqueduct. Luis Manuel beamed as the kid variously peered into five half-submerged tubes.

"These babies look a little rusty," I said.

Luis Manuel scoffed, and with a casual flick of the hand said most of the pipes were old to begin with, and it didn't matter anyhow because all pipes led to Romo.

Luis Manuel questioned the Indian, who answered by slipping headfirst into the middle pipe.

"Oh, sheeeet," Jimmy said, as Luis Manuel waded over to the middle tube. "We better—take this one—feet first, chico. Better to have your feet take those bends than—your goddam cabeza."

Sage advice, since after two seconds, the tube angled down sharply, slammed round a bend and shot us into the darkness at speed. I blindly tried to stay centered on the slime, clutching my gonads, praying I'd find no U-turns or sloppy welds. The kid's screams died off. Then, suddenly, the pipe vanished beneath me, and I tumbled through the darkness ten feet, twenty, God only knows how far to splash into some sort of tank. No sound from the kid. I thrashed for Jimmy and we clasped hands, treading and terrified, only to get whisked into a whirling eye like that in a draining bathtub. We gasped what we reckoned were last breaths as the vortex sucked us down a thin, vertical shaft. In two seconds—which lasted a century—we smacked bottom and were gushed out into a larger pipe, known so only by the more gentle curvature beneath our accelerating gams. Then we pitched down a ramp so steep our arms flew up, and we started racing all over again, only slightly reassured by the stale air and Luis Manuel's distant screams. These shortly gave way to something that sounded like a drumstick raked across a mile-long charrasca, a studdering, wrenching sound we soon matched when we ground across a corrugated stretch that tweaked and pummeled every joint. We slammed into an elbow that knocked me so hard I saw stars despite the total darkness.

The aqueduct was way behind us now, and in total silence we whistled along for several straight miles, regaining some wits, and a numbing terror. Finally, I managed a scream, as did Luis Manuel, somewhere behind, and finally Jimmy and the kid, both well ahead. We were helpless but to course through the darkness. Then, we bruised off a final bend and shot for a pinhole of light. I breathed again, bashed across a final washboard and only half realized my fifteen-foot free fall into more mud than water.

No one could tell how long our ordeal had taken, only that the mud had dried before anyone could rise. I wobbled toward moving water to soak and check for injuries. The kid had a strained neck and didn't know if he was dead or in Patagonia. Luis Manuel rubbed his collarbone and blood trickled from a gash on his chin. Jimmy hobbled around in circles, mumbling about slaying the Cretan Bull, breaking the Diomede Steed, branding the Cattle of Geryon, plus a load of gibberish no one understood. The distant sound of truck horns proclaimed the autopista several miles away. Not a great distance, but we'd be hoofing it naked since the tubes had stripped the trunks off all four of us.

Arkkk!

By: Jeff Bennett

Have you ever watched a special on Sea World? You know, the trained animal shows, where the seal barks and someone throws him a fish. Well, that was me. The seal. But no one was throwing me a fish, and I wasn't really barking.

I probably sounded like I was barking. But, it was just my water-burdened throat fighting with my lungs for a gasp of air. On my second bark I got sucked back down for another thrashing in some river god's washing machine.

It's weird what your mind does while your body goes ass over teakettle through a river's liquid darkness. "Bummer," I thought. "My mom's gonna ask someone what the last thing I said was and they're gonna have to tell her 'ARK!' You know, Mrs. Bennett. Like a seal...'ARK!'"

The parade of cars should've told me something. Here on the Cal Salmon, cars usually make their way upstream in the morning, downstream in the afternoon. Pretty typical stuff. But, today was different. Not only were there more cars on the road than I'd ever seen before, they were all heading in the opposite direction. Downstream. And it wasn't even noon yet.

By the time we reached the put-in at Nordheimer Flat, only a few boaters were left to be found. "What's up?" I asked one of the guides.

"Oh, not much. You gonna run it today?"

"Yeah."

"A bit high for me. Good luck."

I didn't get it. A little bit of brown water and everyone skittered down river like geese heading south. It just didn't figure.

Well, actually it did figure. But I didn't get it. I'd run the Cal Salmon two years earlier at about 4,300 cfs (cubic feet per second). Pretty high water by Cal Salmon standards. In fact, many of the commercial outfitters start canceling trips around 4,200 cfs. But, now the river was running over 7,500 cfs, and, in the midst of the torrential downpour, it was still coming up!

Since the put-in was at a wide, shallow gravel bar, the extra 3,200 cfs didn't look any different than I'd remembered. Not different enough to stop us from getting on the water anyway. We filled our two 14-foot self-bailers with strong paddle crews and headed down river.

It only took about three minutes to figure out why everyone had packed up their rafts and gone home. The river was big. I mean, REALLY BIG!! The Cal Salmon had gone stark raving bonkers. Our raft felt like it was tied to a locomotive that was dragging us downstream at about twenty miles per hour.

"Okay..." I shouted. "This is gonna be Airplane Turn. Paddle hard!"

All of the familiar landmarks were there. The bends in the canyon. The boulders along the banks. But the rapids were gone. The big boulders that formed the Airplane Turn were about six feet underwater. I hadn't even noticed the Maze or Lewis Creek Falls. But, in their place, a long series of tail waves bounced our raft around like a beach ball at a pool party. It was time for a plan.

"Okay everybody. This is way bigger than anything I've seen in here. Plus, we haven't seen anything yet. So, let's get conservative. Avoid the holes. Power up those waves. Be ready to go high side..."

It was a lame plan! But it was the only thing that was going to work. Now, as if to convince myself that we were going to be all right, I started singing out loud: "...the weather started getting rough/the tiny ship was tossed/if not for the courage of the fearless crew/the Minnow would be lost/the Minnow would be lost..."

We whisked through the canyon with lightning speed. Big rapids came and went in a blur of foam and fury. One of the biggest rapids—Cascade—showed up all too fast. Although we had our butts puckered up on those raft tubes like nervous starfish on rocks, I didn't know if the extra bit of suction could beat the wall of water that had to be waiting at the base of the rapid.

At Cascade, the river divides itself between two chutes. The left side provides a boulder maze, requiring a fast left-to-right move at the bottom to avoid being pancaked in either a hole or on a VW sized boulder. The right side is a steep chute. Almost a waterfall. One of those deals where you line up, hang on, and see what happens. But that was at regular water levels. There was nothing regular about the water level we were seeing today.

Rather than chance a blind run, we stopped on the left bank to scout out the rapid. Much to our relief, the river had filled in the worst parts of the drop, making safe passage possible along either route. We headed back to our boats and ferried to the far right bank. Making the final adjustments, we reached the top of the chute along the right wall and hunkered down a bit in the raft. In a flash of white and water, it was all over. We floated free of Cascade and continued on our race track descent toward the take-out.

Next up was Achilles Heel, a long, steep rapid that tended to slam rafts onto a high, banked curve along the right wall, then straight down over a five or six-foot drop into a nasty hole. Again, at medium flows, rafts could make the pull in order to avoid the hole, or simply hit the hole with momentum. But, at higher levels, the hole developed a healthier appetite for synthetic materials. In fact, one raft spent about five exasperating minutes recirculating in the hole when we made the run at 4,300 cfs. Finally, the rafter jumped out of the raft and swam down to an eddy, letting the river bounce the raft around for another few minutes before letting it go.

We were going to creep through the boulders near the top of the rapid, then paddle like hell to avoid the hole. But, somewhere high above us, someone heard our plan and said, "Yeah, sure, watch this fools."

Our raft shot across the rapid like a loose cork from a warm bottle of champagne. We were on an inflatable rocket sled. I didn't even have a chance to say "We're screwed!" before we were perched upon a pillow, high on the right bank, staring straight down into the guts of Achilles Heel.

"FORWARD PADDLE!!!" I guess I should've been honest with my crew. What I really meant was "you guys forward paddle, I'm just going to sit back here and hold on for all I'm worth."

But, everyone knew exactly what I meant, and they weren't about to let me be the only one arm wrestling a safety strap. I mean, this was a perfect opportunity to match grip strength against the best the Cal Salmon had to offer.

We slid a few inches higher on the pillow, then violently changed direction. Sitting in the back of the raft, I felt as if the entire San Francisco 49er's defensive line had landed on me. I couldn't see a thing, but could feel a wall of water wrapping itself around my shoulders and dragging me backwards into the hole. We had slammed the hole with some momentum, but had stalled momentarily. I hung on just long enough to watch the water clear away and my crew paddling furiously into a friendly eddy.

We were almost home. One set of rapids to go. By now, we had figured that we were pretty invincible. We started feeling kind of sorry for all those rafters who had left the river and gone home. This was turning out to be a heck of a good time.

Mile six. Here we are. The granddaddies of all Cal Salmon rapids. Last Chance and Freight Train. Also known as Big Joe or Grant's Bluff depending on who you talk to. This was the original home of whitewater carnage. In fact, Gayle Wilson's two home videos, Whitewater Bloopers I and II, provide hours of entertainment at the expense of countless paddlers who have been thrashed here.

Last Chance gets its name from a big eddy at the bottom right side of the rapid. The idea is to swing around some boulders, start pulling to the right, and avoid the big hole at the base of the rapid. Done correctly, you'll find yourself in a peaceful eddy with a second chance to scout out an even worse Class V rapid downstream...Freight Train. Screw up and you're likely to flip in the hole. Then, that eddy is your last chance to swim to the bank before swimming Freight Train.

I had seen this rapid plenty of times before. I knew its reputation, and had seen the calamities. I had probably been a victim to a calamity there once or twice myself. But, today was going to be different. The rocks on the right bank were totally submerged. We could bounce along the right bank, and take what looked like a highway around the right side of the hole.

What we hadn't accounted for was the fact that our success upstream had pissed off a river god back at Achilles Heel. And there's nothing worse than cheating a river god out of a good flip and swim session. Now it was his chance to show us who was boss.

We took the most enthusiastic paddlers from the two rafts and loaded them into one boat. At the base of Last Chance two people waited with throw bags in case anything went awry. We talked over our paddle itinerary and headed for the current.

Coming around the top of the rapid, it was immediately apparent that something was really wrong. We were way out in the middle of the river. Nowhere near the right bank, as we had planned. The current was much more than we had expected, and we were on a collision course with the big hole.

Rather than succumb to the whims of the river gods, we struggled for the right bank. Big mistake. We hit the hole squarely on our side. I jumped on the downstream tube, took one deep breath, and kissed the daylight good-bye.

It's amazing how little a lifejacket does for you on a flooded river. My feet could have been pointed straight at the surface for all I knew. Still, it feels kind of good to swim like hell. Like you're gonna save yourself or something. Even if you don't know top from bottom.

I popped to the surface and was amazed to find the raft right in my face…with my buddy Doc still hanging on to it. I started to reach for the flip line before I realized where we were. First one rock slammed my leg, then another. We were at the top of Freight Train. I remember saying to myself "this is gonna suck!" then getting a deathgrip on a handle and crossing all of my toes for good luck.

There is nothing in the English language that can describe the violence of a Class V swim. Even holding onto that raft, it was all I could do to prevent being dragged down like a two-ton anchor. Waves buffeted us from all sides. "Have we made it past the big hole?" I silently questioned. I looked skywards toward my angry river god and listened. Combined with the thunder of the whitewater, his answer resounded like a massive whale belch...NOPE!

The pressure was awesome. Try as I did, my grip was sheered from the raft. Leaving the thunder of the surface storm, I entered the dark world of river demons. Rather than fight it, I rolled up into a tight ball, like those cannonball dives that kids do. If I didn't struggle, I could save my oxygen in case I was down long.

Time is a very relative concept, something that your mind tends to screw with when you can't see your watch. Especially when you're in life-threatening situations. As I rolled through the dark bowels of the Cal Salmon, my time and reality had become painfully slow. I wanted to hit the fast forward switch. I wanted to read the end of the book first.

WHOO-O-O—SH! I was jettisoned toward the surface, blasting out of the pillow just before slamming into the walls marking the exit from Freight Train. "ARK!" I snapped a lung full of air and looked to the right. At first I thought it was an illusion. A sick, demented mirage tossed there by my river god. But no, it was real...the raft was within an arm's length of me. I flung my arm toward a handle and breathed a huge sigh of relief.

"ARK!" Well, maybe I breathed too soon.

Like a baby doll being held out a car window, I hung onto the side of the raft, swinging behind it to the safety of the pool below. Soon, Doc and I had the raft flipped back over, and paddled it down to the eddy at Butler Creek take-out.

We decided to head back upstream together to see how the rest of our team was doing. In a few minutes we were standing amidst some rafters staring down at Last Chance and Freight Train from the towering cliffs known as Grant's Bluff.

"Just get off the river?" someone asked.

"Yeah," I said.

"You should have seen this flip a couple of minutes ago! AWE-SOME!"

Before I could respond, my mind flashed back. I was instantly transported back to the bottom of Freight Train. I couldn't breathe. Staring at the rafter in front of me, I struggled, struggled some more, and finally answered...

"A-A-A-ARK!"

Death of a Hair Boater, Perhaps!

By: Ian Black

I have aged enough that the immortality I once thought I had kayaking, as with other pastimes, has vanished. Too many friends have gotten hurt; friends of friends have gotten killed. Perhaps my marriage has made a difference? All my Class V cronies shook their heads at the wedding. I have replaced my cocky invincibility with trying to become an old man of the river—trying to keep a straight face when I say, "I would love to do a first descent, but I have to vacuum today."

I made a lousy river guru. My dramatic near-death experience, which is imperative to every old man of the river, proved so ludicrous no one would have believed it; my in-laws wouldn't have talked to me, my wife would never have forgiven me and my friends would not have accepted it if I had died boating. There are those who would argue dying the day before your wedding is dramatic; I'm afraid I would have to disagree.

Dramatic would have been dying in Corsica or Europe. Dying in the wilderness believing I was Kurtz. Dying on a first descent or saving a buddy. I have done all the above (minus the poetic liberties) and have remained relatively unscathed save for bruises to the

ego and twisted ankles from scouting. Instead, my potential demise proved to be a local river on a rapid I had done before. Even the sun shone merrily instead of being overcast and foreboding.

All of my friends were in town for the wedding. These were the other experts. Friends who I had boated with around the world. No one noticed, or commented, that we had all gotten older, fatter, slower. Some of us were out of shape and hungover; others had not been in their boats for months.

This is why women like my wife fear male bonding. Invariably, as with most male bonding lacking tequila (there had been plenty before and there would be plenty after), there was sport involved. It also had the important feature that the river we were doing was illegal. However, the most important thing was that the infamous Dawgs were back together ready to prove that idiocy need not disappear with senescence and that the group need not accept limitations of age and time. This is not to infer that we were idiots to do this river. Rather, we were idiots to think it was possible to lead a life full of such reunions amidst the obligations we have all incurred.

The river is perfect Class IV boating and just plain beautiful. A couple of Class V drops make it humbling or scary depending on whether one runs the rapid. Mark ran the first serious drop with no mishaps. No problem. This was not the best indicator, however, as Mark boats some of the most difficult rivers in the country with drool on his lips instead of fear in his eyes.

Then, another Mark ran it. Problems. He got trashed and dislocated his shoulder. While I commiserated with him, I did not identify. I was boating well and feeling good. And, while I was to be married the next day, time stood still while I boated with friends who had seen me go over waterfalls, had seen me bang my head into parked vehicles as I raged against the moon, and had seen me grow up.

With the usual pit in my stomach I picked my line and entered the rapid. I paddled right into a hole that rudely informed me and my boat that we weren't going anywhere. After rolling a couple of times and getting nowhere, I started thinking this was a drag. After feeling the boat undulate up and down against an undercut rock, I thought this was now a bigger drag. After exiting my boat, and not getting a breath of air before getting sucked down and pinned at a 45-degree angle against a rock, my thoughts turned to anguish and disbelief.

Perhaps, if I ever have another one of these experiences, it will be peaceful and I will see my life flash before my very own eyes. This was not the case now. All I could think about was how serious the situation was, while the clock kept ticking and my lungs burned in resentment from the lack of oxygen. Somewhere among the cobwebs and hypoxia, I remembered that you're supposed to roll up into a ball if you find yourself stuck beneath an undercut rock; that's what I always read. Hell, that's what I taught my beginner kayak classes. As I scrunched up, however, I became more deeply pinned. With a quarter of the river jamming my face against the rock and curving my back even more, I must have indeed looked like an old man of the river. But, not the kind I wanted to be.

All of my thoughts originated somewhere between the time I got further wedged and when I started working my way out. It was only a couple of seconds at most, yet I thought enough to fill a lazy Sunday. I thought that my body would not be recovered for days, and when it was, it would be bloated beyond recognition. I thought of all my most trusted friends watching and not being able to do anything. I thought that the funeral wouldn't be a problem with everyone already in town for my wedding anyway. I thought of it not being fair. I thought of how people would call me irresponsible when I could have told them I didn't want to die trapped under water. I thought that I would soon pass out.

As much as I would like to boast and say my experience, skill and cool head took over, I really don't think that was the case. More likely, my mind checked out in deference to instinct. I think my body realized that my mind would just get in the way and panic. My body figured that I may as well do something since once I passed out, my options would be limited. Somehow, I managed to reach my upstream arm over my head and start pulling myself downstream along the rock. After a couple of feet of this, I got flushed through a rock tunnel, barely large enough to fit through head first. If I had gotten stuck sideways in the tunnel, both my body and my mind would have checked out forever.

After getting flushed out it still took a few seconds to reach the surface. Even if I pass out now, I thought, my friends can do C.P.R. and the body will be recovered. While maytagging about under the surface, an incredible calm infused me. I reached the surface and my wedding without further mishap.

The nightmares have stopped. I would dream of being pinned and wake up just as I started to pass out. I have even been back in my boat. I stopped looking for deep lessons to be learned some time ago. For awhile I played with the idea that from now on, I would only boat very easy rivers. But the friends I know who have made that decision have stopped boating altogether. The hardest lesson has been that given the chance I would do it all over again. No glaring mistakes in judgment were made. Rather, life and death simply proved more arbitrary than I would care to admit.

Recently, I came across this quote by Helen Keller. If I had found it sooner, it would have saved me much thought.

"Security is mostly a superstition. It does not exist in nature, nor do the children of men as a whole experience it. Avoiding danger is no safer in the long run than outright exposure. Life is either a daring adventure or nothing."

Downunder: An Island to Ourselves

By: Diane Christiansen

Being stranded on a deserted tropical island with your lover is a fantasy many, including Hollywood, have dredged up over the years as a solution for what ails us. My husband Jeff and I were ripe for turning such a fantasy into reality. After all, we hadn't come all the way from California to Australia's Great Barrier Reef to hang out with crowds of other tourists. We definitely needed a change—and soon!

On the morning of the seventh day I was up early for one of my island strolls when I found myself in the company of one worn and weathered local, Captain Brian. He was the owner of an 18 foot tri-maran which he had used to motor visitors around the reef for the past twenty years.

I told him that my husband and I were getting tired of all the tourists, and he responded with an exciting proposition: for a small fee he could take Jeff and I to a "very primitive" island, twenty eight miles south of Dunk and return in two weeks time to take us back to the mainland. Like its owner, the boat wasn't in great shape but, what the heck, the deal sounded affordable and almost too good to be true—a tropical vacation fantasy in the flesh. Enthused and proud of myself for swinging such an adventurous deal, I went back to share our latest good fortune with Jeff...

We spent about $100 stocking up on supplies. I thought it would be fun to finally learn how to fish, so we stuffed some line and hooks into our packs. We bought all our favorite treats. We pictured ourselves laying back and reading for hours, snacking away the days and enjoying intimate moments on our own, personal fantasy island.

It took us a leisurely two and a half days just to reach Hinchenbrook Island, camping on tiny islands that dot the area, some no bigger than a spit of sand and a palm tree. Jeff and I swam and snorkeled along the way, with Captain Brian sailing beside and behind us. Huge sea turtles joined us from the sea grass depths; schools of electric fish darted by; sea eagles soared and dove for fish around us.

One morning, chilled after a two mile swim, we stood in knee deep water on a 25 to 30 foot tall coral bommie, letting the warm sun toast our backs. The water was green and deep around our small platform of coral. Suddenly, a seven foot reef shark shot out at us from below, pulling up short when it was close enough for us to see its tiny eyes. I stopped breathing—adrenaline surged. It suddenly occurred to me that my bright new phosphorescent Nikes looked very much like the parrot fish in these waters. Parrot fish are prey to these sharks. More adrenaline. The shark began circling.

Jeff and I, masks in the water, rear ends high in the air, rotated around and around as we jostled each other to stay on the tiny surface area of our bommie while keeping our eyes on the shark. It circled an agonizing three times before disappearing as abruptly as it had appeared. We left a wake in our hurry to swim back to the boat—snorkeling was definitely over for the day.

We reached our destination not long afterward and it took three trips in a dinghy through small breaking surf to unload all our food and equipment. I had made a tracing of Captain Brian's chart, which showed the outline of the island, including drainages with intermittent fresh water streams, and an "X" marking the spot where Captain Brian said he was "pretty sure" there was an "exclusive resort." By my reckoning, finding the resort would involve a 21 mile trek through a dense rainforest if a real emergency arose.

There really was no need for worrying though. After all, we could expect Captain Brian in two weeks, when our new friend would arrive to spend a few days with us on the island before boating us back to the mainland. We gave him money for his time and some extra funds to purchase the needed supplies we would require for the extra few days on the island once he returned. As Captain Brian sailed off, we waved good-bye and then headed down the beach to find the perfect campsite.

What mattered most during our first few island days was that we were finally alone! We had fun setting up an elaborate "Swiss Family Robinson" camp, and exploring. It was winter in the northeast tropics of Australia. The days were warm and the nights were delightfully cool. We didn't wear any clothing, unless we were hiking, and Jeff made himself a great palm frond hat to keep the burns to a minimum.

Days were as you would imagine, filled with reading, eating, collecting shells, bodysurfing, exploring fresh water streams and waterfalls, and hiking to the ends of our mile-long white sand beach. We discovered tracks of Australia's giant five foot long Goanna lizards and watched the cockatoos, bright and wild against the dark green rainforest. We also talked for long hours and days, about our pasts, our families, and how we wanted our future together to be.

We sat under our tarps and watched how the sea changed with the coming of each warm afternoon squall. We noticed how the waves would come in bigger and faster, and how the water would get cloudy before each squall hit. We were absolutely alone and loving it. We had a lot of time.

After Day 9 on the island we joked about the possibility of actually becoming stranded on this island—kind of a Robinson Crusoe situation for real. Although we both knew that kind of event only happened in movies, we started planning for a worst-case scenario. We took stock of our supplies and discovered that we were already a bit low. We decided we'd better start rationing and try our luck at fishing. We stowed away a couple of cans of food for the hike out, just in case.

We started fishing. I got frustrated easily. Jeff was patient. He caught tasty fish from our lagoon right away. It was good to know that if we really had to, we could catch fish.

We also found about five good coconuts that the bush rats hadn't found first. They tasted great. Another good food, should we really need it.

By Day 14, our supplies were nearly depleted. I was losing weight and for the first time in my life not enjoying it. Fishing started consuming most of our waking interest and time although this incessant practice, for me, did not improve my skill.

Two days later, sitting by a deep tide pool, I caught a lobster quite by accident. It put up an amazing fight to survive. I struggled with the "beast" until Jeff arrived, to find me hunched over and beating the hell out of a crustacean—he actually had to pull me off of it to get me to stop. The situation was beginning to feel serious, and still there was no sign of Captain Brian.

After the lobster episode I stopped trying to fish altogether. I discovered oysters and spent my days gathering. It is a feeling I will never forget: waking up in the early morning, hunger gnawing at my insides, and hiking off to the oyster beds to gather as many oysters as possible before high tide. We ate an estimated 10 kilos of oysters in all. There was no more time or energy for reading, lolling, and exploring; we were focused on the basics. While I gathered, Jeff hunted—both of us with our eyes searching the horizon for Captain Brian.

On Day 21 Jeff sliced his toe on a rock. We knew that infections in the tropics set in fast, so we decided to try to reach the "pretty sure it was there" resort. We had given up on Captain Brian's return.

The next morning, we checked my tracing of Captain Brian's chart. Finding fresh water was a question in our minds and from earlier explorations we knew that the shoreline was extremely rocky, so it would be slow going. After pondering the map for awhile we thought we could save maybe seven to ten miles off the estimated 21 if we took a short cut through the rainforest estuary, rather than follow the coastline all the way around to the north end of the island. Jeff and I were experienced hikers and could handle any terrain, or so we thought...

It was a particularly hot day, and feeling weakened by weight loss and by our overloaded backpacks we pushed our way inland for almost four hours. We were moving as fast as possible because we were unsure of just about everything; where we were headed, when we would find fresh water again, and how long it was going to take to get to the "resort." Adding to our misery were the razor sharp palm vines we had to contend with.

I was sweating profusely and exhausted when I slid down an embankment and was suddenly jerked to a stop by a complicated mesh of "lawyer vines" (so called because they will grab at you and keep you all tangled up for ages). Hanging there suspended, I felt like a bug in an immense spider web. I made some joke about finally getting to use the saw blade on my Swiss Army knife. It was an absurd (but typical) attempt to keep our spirits up, and Jeff probably could have done without the cheerleader routine.

Before I tell you what happened next, I'd like to share with you some relevant tidbits regarding Australia's insecta—in particular, green ants. They are the size of black carpenter ants, with transparent green abdomens, and are so aggressive that the presence of larger mammals passing near a branch on which they are crawling triggers a jump and attack response. Their bite is so tenacious that brushing against their bodies causes their heads to be left imbedded in the flesh.

So, no shit...there I was, laughing uproariously for good effect and sawing away, shaking the entire rainforest around me. It was then that the unbelievable happened: a nest of angry, swarming green ants fell on my neck. I lost it completely!

I screamed and screamed some more, all while ripping and tearing myself free of the vines. Jeff tore off my pack and shirt and slapped at the ants while I tried to keep them from crawling into my eyes, nose, ears and mouth. Jeff's horrified look didn't exactly help to calm the situation any, but time passed in some unreal way and finally, at last, the biting stopped.

Though green ants are not poisonous and the pain of their bite didn't last long (only the memory) this episode was the last straw. We gave up on the short cut and turned back to the coast. We would now face the grueling miles of rocky cliffs.

On the third morning of our foot journey—24 days after our arrival on the island—we discovered a trail leading up from the beach. And, there, before our eyes and most definitely not an apparition was a man approaching, obviously well fed and relaxed. This was it! We were saved!

We could hardly wait to greet the man, tell him what had happened, capture him with the essence of our arduous saga and watch his eyes bug out in disbelief. We eagerly approached him and began spilling our story. He took his time looking us over. He listened a while. Then, he turned away, uttering in apparent disgust just one word: "Yanks."

Epilogue:

Well, we got off the island without further mishap. The resort was down the trail a little ways. We had to hike over the airstrip to get to the palm-lined swimming pools and cool drinks. Sure, we didn't look much like exclusive resort guests—tired, sweaty, dirty, and schlepping packs—but the resort treated us well, even if our initial encounter wasn't exactly brimming with friendship. After recounting our story, much to the disbelief of our hosts, we were told that the estuary we had initially planned to cross (before the ants turned us back) was brimming with saltwater crocodiles. Terrific.

What ever happened to Captain Brian? We never knew. He could have been lost at sea or in a good drunken stupor somewhere. He could have just ripped us off. All in all, we wish him well.

I still fantasize about my personal island paradise. Maybe someday I'll go back. I imagine Jeff would head off to an island paradise again too, but this time with crates of food, nearby room service and a guaranteed trip off the island.

Walking on the Wild Side with Our President

By: Michael Hodgson

When I received a phone invitation to go on a hike through the Giant Sequoias in California with President Bush during the Fall of 1992, my initial reaction was, "Right, who is this, really?" I could name any number of wonderful friends who would make such an "official" offer while doubled up with mirth and glee—eager to hang any appearance of gullibility over my head for a lifetime. "Honest, this really is the White House Press Office," asserted the caller, seeming somewhat irritated at my disbelief.

As it turned out, I really was to be one of only six outdoor journalists selected to join the President for a few quiet moments and a private audience prior to his signing a proclamation to preserve the Sequoias (quiet and private in a President's case means any group gathering of under 100 people—not including Secret Service).

"Honey, I have been invited to go on a private walk with the President," I proudly proclaimed to my wife that evening after dinner.

"That's nice dear...did you remember to call the dentist today?"

My wife's lack of enthusiasm notwithstanding, I knew that such an honor called for nothing less than my best backpacking T-shirt,

one without holes of course, and my cleanest pair of hiking boots. Secrecy, for obvious reasons, shrouded the visit. I had been told to drive to Bakersfield, California, where our chosen group of journalists would get instructions as to where to rendezvous with drivers who would escort us to the President and his chosen trail. I wonder if he has to stand in line like the rest of us for a permit? Probably not.

Secret Service were everywhere in the hotel. Not that they necessarily wanted you to notice. After all, they were wearing nifty disguises that were their version of what press should look like, complete with khaki vests, comfortable shoes and nattily pressed slacks. The major difference between them and us, however, was that the bulges in their vests were a little more deadly than the Nikons and tape recorders the authentic press were toting.

The phone call came through late that night detailing final instructions, complete with inexplicable static (were their official ears listening in?). At 6:30 a.m. we clambered into two Isuzu Troopers—hmmm, driving in a Japanese vehicle to visit an American President when everyone is clamoring "buy American?" Interesting election-year strategy! Still, we arrived at the first checkpoint without incident—perhaps that explains the vehicle choice.

There, we were greeted by the U.S. Forest Service's (USFS) finest, complete with no sense of humor—apparently a requisite if you are to provide security for the President. The other requirement, as I was to discover, is to act as if you have no idea what is going on.

Checkpoint two was staffed by a California Highway Patrol (CHP) officer who had obviously practiced his saunter and was going to milk his moment for all it was worth. Still, two minutes to walk 20 feet is a bit much and, if he is reading this (and you know who you are), lose the shades; they look too cliché. After a minute or two of consultation, we were waved down a dirt road to an operational headquarters at R.M. Pyles Boys Camp.

More of the same. Blank stares from Secret Service, USFS, and a litany of local law all of whom operated under the same code for the day—everything is on a need-to-know basis, and we have no idea what it is we need to know regarding your visit. Finally, after 30 minutes of standing around wondering what was next and if the President was going to come and go without us, someone who knew who we were finally arrived. Back in the Isuzus and up to the CHP officer who had, in the space of 30 minutes, forgotten he had ever seen us.

I'll say this much for him—he had a great saunter. Mr. CHP was yet another one of the majority who apparently didn't need to know anything, so he had to call someone who did. That person arrived. He was Secret Service from his head to his jockey shorts—shades, short hair, chiseled looks, and lips that were trained to remain straight and never reveal any emotion (these guys have just got to be a thrill-a-minute at social functions). He waved us on.

Several more checkpoints and we arrived. We were hustled through a metal detector (bet you didn't know they have those at trailheads now, did you?) and had our gear checked for weapons (although in all the clamor, my large camera bag was never scanned or peeked into, not once. Great security guys!). Finally, our little group of bleating journalists was herded down a trail to a point where we were told to wait for the President.

Tom Clancy once said that the Secret Service owned the night. It looked as if they owned the trees, the trail and the sky as well. In fact, I wouldn't swear to this, but some of those trees and large boulders appeared to be watching us through riflescopes. This was not the weekend to plan a casual picnic with the family in Sequoia National Park.

Suddenly, we experienced a minor group panic, led of course by the previously calm Presidential aide. "Where's Pat!?" Apparently my good friend and renowned outdoor humor writer Patrick McManus was no longer with our group. I'm not absolutely sure, but I thought I heard several hundred safeties being clicked off as Secret Service scopes and rifle sights began scanning the trail for a subversive humorist.

Fortunately, Pat has vast experience at being lost, almost more than I, and upon noticing he had become separated from our herd, he executed his patented "Modified Stationary Panic" until the Presidential aide, who was executing a version of fully mobile panic, found him. Pat shook off the entire incident with a chuckle—the Secret Service, on the other hand, was not laughing. Some people have no sense of humor.

In strode the President, surrounded by an entourage that included former Secretary Baker and his wife, EPA head Reilly, USFS head Robertson, and others. Even more Secret Service with their deadpan faces scurried in, one of whom carried a large pack (internal frame, in case you care) complete with antennae—can you say "nuclear launch?" This was like no other wilderness hike I had ever been on.

A firm handshake and a warm greeting for each of us, and we were off walking through the forest with the President. The President gazed at carefully chosen natural landmarks that included several very large Sequoias. We gazed (at the President gazing) at trees. The President walked, we walked. The President stopped, we stopped. I was beginning to feel a bit like a Presidential groupie.

What did the President say that was memorable you ask? Hmmm. Other than defending his environmental record at every opportunity (we are still searching for actual evidence of that record) he did make reference to God being an arsonist. Say what? Yep. He said, after asking the USFS silviculturist about USFS policy on controlling forest fires, that he had heard, "Lightning starts many fires which means that God is an arsonist and that is why the forest looks so good." Interesting concept Mr. President—quick Barbara, hide the matches.

We also discovered, under heavy questioning by a relentless outdoor press corps, that the President loves fishing, had just taken up fly fishing but wasn't very good yet, and that he runs a nine-minute mile. Critical election year material, which may partially explain November 1992's final election-night tally.

All in all, the day was most pleasant. I would do it again in a heartbeat. So it is when you get invited to go wandering with the Commander-in-Chief of our country. Perhaps most rewarding was observing Secretary Baker and his wife eagerly smelling the vanilla bark of a Jeffrey pine, picking up pine cones with fascination, and generally being the only members of the Presidential party who seemed to be truly aware of what this walk really meant—a brief moment of peace in an otherwise frenetic world.

Just before the President was hustled off to deliver his proclamation before the White House Press Corps, we outdoor journalists had our pictures taken with him—probably the main reason any of us were there, to be honest.

Oh, one final note. As we were leaving, the radio aboard a USFS truck crackled, announcing that a convoy of five CHP cars were lost on a remote logging road and couldn't turn around (so much for that shortcut). I presume that they eventually got things sorted out, but in case you come across a group of humbled officers while hiking among the Sequoias, point them in the right direction will you—President Clinton may be looking for them.

A Bear Story

By: Jim Ward

I've only told this story a handful of times—it's not an easy story to tell. It's a bit emotional for me when I look a great while back and think about that August day. My father liked to fish up in Alberta, Canada. There's a nice river up there that he would swear by for its good fishing. It was a long drive and at times I wonder how we ever made it. The roads were bad and often there were no roads at all. After the drive, a two-day hike would put us into the back country and to the special spot Dad liked to go. If he could, he would have gone there every year. As it was, this was our last time.

I was eleven years old then. We were camping not too far from the river, and it was a beautiful summer day. We had been there a few days and my dad had caught a number of fish. Everything was perfect. I remember wanting to go on a day hike by myself. My dad said okay and not to go too far. I loved to explore new surroundings, my heart being full of adventure.

I crossed the river very patiently, boulder by boulder, making it across and going up the opposite bank several hundred yards. I scampered up a long hill and found myself on the edge of a beautiful meadow surrounded by woodland. There were a few alders in the middle of it. I was having a great time, it was warm and I could feel the sun on my back. As I walked across the meadow I found an old abandoned beehive, an old mud-type hive, the kind that are

67

usually pictured in storybooks. It was full of honeycomb inside. I thought to myself—no bees! So, I stuck the honeycomb and hive into my daypack next to my lunch. I couldn't wait to see the look on my dad's face when I showed him my great find.

After sticking the honeycomb in my pack, I started off back towards camp. Not paying much attention to anything, out of the corner of my eye I saw something move over on the edge of the woods. I turned around, looked, and I didn't see anything but a meadow full of wildflowers. I stared for a while, thinking I startled a deer or something. I turned around and started off. Again, I thought I saw something move. I wasn't real sure and I turned around. Right there on the edge of the forest was a large bear. I didn't know what kind, grizzly or black, male or female. All I knew was that it was a bear! A chilling fear crept over me. I didn't want to act afraid, I knew from the things that my dad had told me that I should act calm. I knew bears were fast and I knew that a bear could outrun me very easily.

Not too far away from me was a small stand of trees, alder, I' guess. I'm not really sure what they were, but they were in the middle of the meadow—three or four of them clumped together. I thought if I could only make it to those trees, then maybe I could climb one. I remembered grizzly bears couldn't climb. Not knowing what kind this one was, I didn't want to take any chances. He was big and that's all I needed to know. I figured that I was closer to the tree and could get there faster than the bear if it decided to come after me. I remember counting, "one, two, three, GO." I ran as hard and as fast as I could. It seemed like those trees were so far away. In reality, they were not more than a hundred feet distant. The bear was on the other side of the meadow, at least 200 yards beyond the trees. As soon as I got to the trees, I wheeled around. I could see the bear lumbering toward me, not really fast, but not slowly, that was for sure. I knew I had no time to waste. The trees weren't that big around, six or seven inches in diameter. I straddled my legs around the first one I came to. The lowest branch was almost too high—I could just reach it. I pulled myself up and got my knees over the branch. Struggling, I finally got up onto that first branch. After that, I climbed on up fairly easily. The branches were close enough together, enabling me to scramble up the tree in the nick of time.

The bear came charging up and came to a stumbling stop underneath me, sending earth and flowers flying. The bear snorted and was breathing heavily. At that point I could tell he was a grizzly. As I looked at that big hump on his back my fear increased. The bear stood up and started clawing at the tree—I guess to see if he could reach me. He was only a foot or two beneath my feet as he reared up standing on his hind legs.

As the weight of the predicament I was in settled on my shoulders, I began to feel very alone and very lost—possibly this was to be my end. This was the first time that I had ever thought as a child that maybe I could die, and it seemed really grim at this point to think about being killed by a bear. There I was, up in a tree with a bear pawing at the trunk, grunting and snorting.

Before long, I realized that I had wet my pants. The breeze blowing through the trees made me feel very cold all of a sudden. I wondered what was going to happen. The bear got back down and walked away from the tree, then came back, turning his head from side to side. One or two more times he reared up on his hind legs and tried to reach me before finally deciding that he couldn't. Feeling a little secure, I thought about screaming for my father. I began yelling and screaming, in a panic almost, until I became hoarse and couldn't scream anymore. Nobody came. I hadn't realized that the sound of the river would probably drown out any noises that I could have made.

Then, suddenly, it dawned on me that in my day pack was the honeycomb and hive. I realized that maybe it wasn't me the bear wanted all of this time. I quickly tried to take the pack off, and as I did it became caught in the branches. The harder I tried to remove the pack, the more entangled it became. After quite a struggle, I managed to dump the hive and honeycomb down onto the ground for the bear. He licked it, and pawed it a little, but seemed really uninterested in it. This was very confusing to me because I had always thought that honey was a bear's favorite food. I knew now that it was me this bear was preoccupied with. I wasn't sure if it was just curious or what it was up to. I just wished he would leave.

It seemed like hours had passed by. Finally, the bear seemed to give up and just walk away, slowly. He walked about halfway from the trees to the edge of the meadow, turned and looked, then dropped his head and lumbered towards the forest. In another minute he was out of sight. I thought I had better wait a while before climbing down.

The trees were in the middle of the meadow and I knew that it was a few hundred yards to the other side of the meadow before I could get to the woods to another tree and to a possible place of safety if the bear should appear again. I waited as long as I could before I thought I'd go crazy. What seemed like hours was in reality probably 10 to 15 minutes. I slowly started climbing down out of that tree. It was the most frightening experience, getting back down on the ground where the bear had just been, but I knew that I had to do it. I had to get out of that tree and back to camp and the only way I was going to accomplish this was to get moving. It was around noon and my father didn't really expect me back until around four or so—too long to wait around for him to come looking for me.

There I was, climbing down on the ground with a sense of relief and terror all at once. I thought I would walk slowly to not attract attention while in the meadow and once in the woods, run quickly to camp. As I planned, I started off slowly. Suddenly, something made me look toward the edge of the woods. Ahead of me loomed the same bear—I froze in terror. Every hair on my body stood on end as any sense of relief I had been feeling quickly vanished. I was absolutely petrified. I didn't know what to do.

The bear was now 200 yards away and was looking right at me. He had circled all the way around the meadow and was on the side in the direction that I needed to go. The bear raised into the air and sniffed. I figured he couldn't see me very well and was checking my scent. The only thing I could think to do was run for a tree not too far away from the stand I had just left. As I was thinking, the bear started towards me. Instantly, I turned and started running towards that tree—I knew it was going to be close. There were just seconds to get into that tree before it would be all over. I was 175 to 200 feet away. Recalling back, running to the tree seemed an eternity—like a dream when someone is chasing you and you cannot move. Muscles somehow freeze up on you, and whatever is after you finally overcomes you. Only, this wasn't a dream, this was real—the most terrifying moments in my entire life. Adrenaline pumping, I started climbing, pulling myself up and hooking my legs over a branch. In between movements, I caught a glimpse of that bear thundering towards me—just a few feet away. It was an incredible sight.

The ground was shaking. I continued climbing, desperately. Some of the branches broke off and I began to feel like I wasn't going anywhere. The branches were thick and I became tangled, poking myself in the eye. I was confused and yet I knew I had to keep clawing, climbing, anything to get out of reach of that bear. The bear stood up and clawed at me, catching my pant leg, almost jerking me out of the tree. I lost my balance, then regained it, pulling my leg away quickly. Then, I pulled my legs up under me and clung to the tree and cried—tears streaming down my face—I was absolutely terrified. I was just inches out of the bear's reach. He started making an awful bawling noise and other sounds that sent chills and goose bumps all over my body. I think most people tend to think of bears as cuddly creatures, growling fiercely only when they are angry, but never could I imagine the kinds of sounds that were coming from this animal.

The bear started pushing on the tree and shaking it. Then, he would jump down onto his forefeet, stomp around the tree to the other side and stand up again. He seemed to be very enraged. Why, I didn't know. I suppose I was infringing upon his territory; whatever it was, the bear was apparently very furious with me.

I screamed and was crying, wanting help, pleading for my father to come. I kept on screaming and pleading until I felt exhausted. My screaming only enraged the bear more. Though I became sure that no one was coming, screaming was all I felt I had left to do.

Everything was hopeless—I knew that if the bear went away and I got out of the tree, he would be waiting for me. I sobbed to the point where the tears ceased to come down my cheeks anymore. I remember thinking that if I just sat there long enough, my father might realize that I was in trouble and would come looking for me.

With that thought, I relaxed some and just hugged onto the tree, waiting. The bear, on the other hand, didn't have waiting in mind. He started chewing on the bark of the tree, scratching it with his claws and pushing on it with his paws. The meadow was a little soggy and moist in that area and the tree wasn't that big—six or seven inches in diameter at the base and only 15 to 20 feet high. I was up near the top, swaying back and forth. I felt like I was on the end of a fishing pole.

I looked at the blue sky and the white clouds, gazed at the meadow and the grass blowing gently with the wind, then focused on the bear. The contrast was overwhelming. What started out to be such a beautiful day was now a living nightmare. This bear was relentless and was now actually pushing and butting the tree with his shoulder and side. He was shaking the daylights out of me. I was having a hard time hanging on—it took every ounce of energy I had just to cling to the tree. I thought several times that maybe I wouldn't make it. Only eleven years old and thinking my number was up. I saw all eleven years flash before my eyes—even at that age, I remember flashing on things so very quickly.

My attention was returned to my immediate situation by a very violent shake; I was feeling warm, cold, terrified and my pants were still very wet. By now the bear was actually getting the tree to lean over in that boggy meadow. I realized that I would be like a weight on a fishing pole, dangling as bait. My arms ached from holding on so tight. I couldn't relax, especially when I envisioned what might happen if I let go. The bear kept on grunting and snarling and pushing and finally stood up to put all of his weight on one side of the tree, causing it to list over at a considerable angle.

The tree began to really sag over at this point and I knew my time was near. I struggled, hanging on, trying to stay on top of the tree. As the tree started angling over even more, I climbed up higher which only caused the tree to bend even lower. Now, I was within reach of the bear and it only took the bear a few seconds to realize it. I remember the bear taking a swipe at me and catching my shirt. The next thing I knew, I was on the ground, underneath the bear. Looking up, I saw his teeth and bristly hair, the saliva and foam in his mouth, and the fine texture of his nose. All of those things were very vivid. I immediately turned over on my stomach and placed my arms protectively as I could, with my elbows against my sides. I felt the bear's warm tongue on me, then his jaws around my head. I never felt any pain and the next thing I knew, he had grabbed my leg between his jaws and was dragging me away. He dragged me 50 feet or so before stopping for some unknown reason. I had struggled the entire time to keep my arms against my side to protect myself.

Suddenly, that bear began to do something that grizzly bears never do. He started to eat me and before too long I was all gone—bones and all—no shit!

Old Nick

By: Linda Navroth

Old Nick was a big, mean fish. My friend Rich and I named him after Nicodemus, the devil himself. He lived in a place we called The Hell Hole (so named for obvious reasons) on Salmon Creek. It was a big, deep pool, loaded with big rocks, a submerged stump, and lots of fallen branches.

We'd been after Nick for three years and had both lost a jillion flies and leaders in that pool because Nick would head for the nearest obstacle when hooked and break you clean off. That fish must have had more hardware hanging on his jaw than a teenager with braces.

As I said, he was a big fish—a huge brown trout, a good thirty inches, and weighing eight to ten pounds, maybe more. It was hard to say for sure. We'd only seen glimpses, mostly in the late evening, while he was snaggling low flying bats in mid-air as they darted over the water. Yep, he was a monster all right, a regular "Jaws." I always heard that ominous music in my head whenever I saw him feeding.

Old Nick's penchant for bats is what finally got Rich to thinking. We'd tried every tempting fly we knew, from huge, black stoneflies to elaborate minnow imitations. We won some, we lost some. When we did connect, Nick broke us off. But, when we saw Old Nick snag a bat for the first time, we knew just what kind of mean, old fish we were dealing with: he was a voracious carnivore, not unlike a bass in his feeding habits.

So Rich went to work at the fly-tying vise and tied the most radical fly I'd ever seen. He started with a light wire 2/0 hook, to which he added a deer hair and marabou feather body, alternating the materials in layers along the hook shank. At about a quarter of the way to the hook eye, he tied in a pair of short, outstretched wings fashioned out of lacquered tissue paper. You'd have had to have seen it to believe it. It looked like a bat!

It's awesome, isn't it?" he asked proudly, gliding it through the air in his hand like a kid playing with a toy airplane.

"Yes, but will it fly?" I asked.

"Oh, ye of little faith," he said, grabbing his fly rod as he headed out the backdoor to the yard.

After half an hour and several near-misses (his head and mine), Rich finally figured out that if he kneeled on the ground, used a short, stout leader, and false cast with slow, wide loops, he could get this unwieldy-looking fly to sail just about three or four inches above the ground. It was uncanny and not a little scary.

The moment of truth was two days later on Salmon Creek. We came up late in the day and it had been threatening to rain all afternoon. The cumulus clouds scudded across the sky like big, gray-bottomed battleships, piling up darkly to the north.

"Are you sure we should do this today?" I asked meekly. Call me a wuss. I like to fish as much as anyone, but I refuse to be a human lightning-rod.

"You're not going to chicken out on me now, are you?" Rich asked in a mock accusatory way.

"Not me," said I, trying to buck up and sound brave. "I'll be with you every step of the way."

"You had me worried there for a moment. Thought you were going to let a little weather scare you off."

"Not me," I repeated, trying sincerely to mean it.

"I'm going to get that fish today and I need you to take the picture," Rich said confidently. "Today we'll make history."

We walked quietly to The Hell Hole, treading lightly so as not to give away our approach. The clouds had moved in quickly and it was getting very dark. The first rumbling of thunder hurried our steps.

As we came to the pool, we stooped low and stayed well back from the bank, ducking behind trees like Indians surrounding the settler's cabin, signaling each other, in full stealth mode.

Rich finally squatted down behind a small boulder at the head of the pool. From here he had a bat's eye view of Old Nick's domain, especially the fallen log laying half in the water that Nick used for his lair. I stayed back behind a tree, camera poised at the ready.

As we waited, a hatch came off the water and the air was suddenly filled with tiny mayflies. This, in turn, brought on the bats, which was like ringing the dinner bell for Old Nick. We could see the shadow of his great bulk move out slowly from under his log.

He moved through the water like a miniature submarine, his dorsal fin just breaking the surface. A bat dipped low over the water. Too low. Bam! Old Nick surged out of the water like a piscine missile and snagged it, splashing back down into the water like a bowling ball.

Rich turned around, looked at me, and gave me his "now-I'm-going-to-kick-some-serious-butt" grin.

As I advanced the film lever to get ready, a bolt of lightening crackled overhead, the thunder crashing at the same time, vibrating my chest cavity. I dropped the camera. Thank God for neck straps.

"Shit!" Rich hissed.

We both looked at the pool, expecting the worst. But, Old Nick wasn't even phased by all the light and noise. He was still cruising and even snatched another bat as we watched.

Rich launched his bat fly quickly. He looked awkward at first, like a kid trying to get a kite up without wind. But soon he was throwing those slow, wide loops he'd practiced and the bat fly skimmed smartly over the water.

Old Nick cruised over toward the gliding fly, leapt out of the water, and grabbed the fly without hesitation. Rich set the hook perfectly on the take and Nick took the fly and most of Rich's line downstream like a runaway freight train. Line screamed off Rich's reel like a banshee.

It was raining now. Big, fat drops splashed down, pebbling the surface of the water. He couldn't see Nick anymore. The only clue to his whereabouts was Rich's rod tip, seriously bent, almost to the butt. His flyline was gone and he was well into the backing.

"Don't let him get to the stump!" I yelled, as if I needed to remind him. I felt helpless. Even though I knew it was Rich's battle all the way, my dreams hung on this fish, too. I wanted to do something.

Rich charged into the water and tried to follow Nick downstream. The thunder roared and the rain increased its fury. I followed as fast as I could nearly taking a header when I slipped on some moss.

After what seemed like hours, Rich finally wore Nick out. He'd led us on a merry chase but all of a sudden he just gave up. Rich kept his line tight and rod tip up as he eased Nick into his landing net. We'd been right. He was a huge fish. He barely fit in the net; a great deal of his tail hung outside of it.

Rich was elated and out of breath. He climbed up onto a flat rock near the bank, holding the fish aloft, straining under the weight.

"Take a picture! Quick!" he shouted. "Man, he's heavy!"

I raised the camera and had my finger on the shutter release when all of a sudden a bolt of lightning snaked out of the darkness and zapped right next to where Rich stood.

He flew backwards off the rock. The fish went one way, his rod the other. The concussion knocked me on my butt in midstream.

When my eyes readjusted and I could see again, I looked for Rich. He was across the stream, in front of me, lurching to his feet, his hair kind of smoking and his eyes wild. He looked like Wyle E. Coyote after sitting on the Roadrunner's dynamite whoopee cushion.

"Son-of-a-Bitch!" Rich growled hoarsely. He was obviously okay, though a little crisp around the edges. I looked over to where his rod lay fractured on some streamside rocks. Old Nick was nowhere to be seen.

"Sorry, buddy," I said sheepishly, not wanting to piss him off anymore than he undoubtedly was. "Looks like your rod is history. And it looks like the fish is too."

Rich looked at me incredulously, his eyes growing wider, more mad. "Screw the rod! To hell with the fish! Did you get the damn picture or not?!" he shouted, his whole body shaking.

Until that moment it hadn't occurred to me to see if I even had the camera around my neck. I looked down at my chest and there it was, safe, and I hoped, sound. I lifted the camera up and tried the shutter release. It clicked.

Blues Above Bishop

By: Ken Winkler

Frank, you see, wasn't a minimalist, especially when it came to backpacking.

"No reason for me to eat dog food when I'm that high up," he said before we started a week trip in the eastern Sierra.

We were headed for Lamark Col, a barren, jagged, incredibly steep, and without trails, cross-country pass. At one point a hiker has to crawl from one hummock to another before he can go upright again. Just the stuff for a minimalist. The drama isn't restricted to the pass itself—the surrounding country presents stark beauty with weather-shattered rock, snow, and a lake that has some of the coldest water this side of ice.

Frank moseyed over to the Safeway in Bishop to "check out what was on sale." Pete and I looked at each other, wondering what he meant. At our feet were the usual freeze-dried meals, cheese, jerky, dried cereals, raisins and nuts. It's what we always packed, but this trip was a first adventure for Frank—casual artist, former university professor and now almond farmer near Sacramento.

"You think he's going to do something stupid?" I asked.

"Like what?"

"Like buy too much!"

"He's got to carry it," Pete mumbled, sorting through his "too heavy" stuff sacks, trying to pare down even more.

It was the same every year. For months he would plot and plan our meals even before we decided where to go. Our packs clung to us like monkeys, there was so little in them they felt terminal. Socks, stove, sleeping bag, food—what else did we need?

Thirty minutes later, Frank returned, his arms wrapped around two huge shopping bags. Frank is a big man, somewhere in the vicinity of 250 pounds and very little of it fat. But, with his mournful expression, his golfer's hat and his long, dirty brown ski parka, which he wore all the time, he looked every bit like a refugee Russian soldier.

"Let's see, now," he began, dropping his bags and pulling off his hat. "Boy, it's hot."

"What's all this shit?" Pete asked.

"Well..." he began, smiling crookedly, his sentence trailing off. Direct answers were not Frank's forte, not after twelve years in the university jungles. "Look here!" He hefted a large head of lettuce out of the first sack. "Only forty cents, that's better than home— check this out!" His arm disappeared into the paper bag. Mumbling, he rummaged around, tossing aside two large loaves of Wonderbread. "This is a real deal—after the ham, that is," he bragged, and held up a huge can of Dinty Moore beef stew. "Can you imagine what this will taste like up there?"

"Better than down here, I hope," Pete said under his breath.

"You guys can eat like squirrels if you like, I'm not," Frank protested, hoisting out a large jar of peanut butter. "Regular butter's gonna melt, so this will do," he announced finishing by grabbing a six-pack of Coca-Cola and kicking the sack aside.

"Are you going to carry all that?" Pete asked, suddenly realizing that Frank was serious.

"Sure am. What did you think I brought this big frame pack for?" Frank looked concerned. "Did I do something wrong?"

"Wrong? No, no, not wrong..." Pete had a pained expression on his face, trying hard to be diplomatic. Outside of a shot of whiskey at night, his idea of a mountain meal was something that didn't weigh over a pound and took less than five minutes to cook.

"But—that—does—look—like—uhhh—it's—uhh—heavy?"

"Oh! We can eat the stew tonight, that's the heaviest. I'll probably go through the first six-pack myself."

"The first?"

"To tell the truth, I bought two of them, just in case." He looked so sheepish, I felt bad. Glancing down at the high-tech food I'd spent so much time agonizing over, I nudged them with my toe. They didn't weigh much, but they suddenly didn't look all that appetizing either.

Frank, meanwhile, had opened his large frame pack and was throwing everything from the shopping bags inside. There was no rhyme or reason to his packing. "Plastic bags—no they can wait. The sweater, that can be wrapped around the ham—almost forgot!" From his jacket he pulled out a big bag of hard candy and dropped it into a side pocket.

He saw me staring at him. "That first pass is a lulu, you know. This is for energy..." and he lapsed into a monologue about how he hated having bad breath, being dehydrated, etc.

"Energy," I repeated. The first pass wasn't difficult, I'd been over it before. I could see Frank tripping under all that crap he was carrying, falling down a thousand feet. The mayonnaise was the worst. It didn't take much imagination to see Frank finally coming to a stop on the rocks at the bottom of Bishop Pass covered with sandwich makings.

"Ready?" Frank stared at us, his one good eye squinting into the bright mid-day light. "I mean, you guys, let's go!"

"Go," was the last word we ever expected from Frank. On the passes during the hike, Frank would disappear from sight after beginning a climb, only to arrive in camp long after the tent was pitched and our boots were off. Ready? Go? Right! His color changed constantly all week as Frank puffed, wheezed and actually gained weight. All those cans and jars just changed location—from the outside to his inside. Nothing Frank did, even scrambling up small rock faces on our days off, seemed to have any effect on his waist.

Many things Frank did during the trip left Pete with a glazed look and his mouth twitching. The top of Lamark was one of those times. The pass was a knife blade, and resting places were few and far between. Also, we weren't alone. At least a dozen others from some climbing school were scattered among the rocks, admiring the view—spectacular to say the least. Not only were the central Sierra visible, but also the White Mountains of east Bishop and the northern end of Owens Valley. Occasional murmurs of appreciation from the other travelers drifted our way as they parceled out their trail mix and salami, munching happily. Then Frank appeared.

After seven days on the trail, his color had stabilized and his hands no longer shook. Even though he constantly brought up the rear, nothing fazed him. Frank liked everything—except for the uphill sections. A "lulu" was a bad one, and a "Well, I dunno" meant he could tackle it, and a "Jeeze Louise!" labeled the climb as tough.

"Mighty fine, mighty fine, but I don't want to do that one again," he said, stopping in the middle of the pass and removing his pack. "Hmmm, snow," he added, glancing towards the crusty drifts that covered the northern exposures.

"I hate the stuff. That will be interesting . . . yes, very interesting." The other travelers stared at him as Frank rubbed his hands and announced he was going to have lunch.

Out came the checkered table cloth which he snapped open and placed on a nearby rock. Scouring further, he produced the mayonnaise, the mustard and some horseradish—lining them up on a flat rock shelf.

"Hey, guys, the lettuce is still good." Heads jerked around when he produced the badly wilted remains.

A loaf of Wonderbread joined the condiments. "One good thing about this one, is that you never have to worry about it drying out. I'm talking basic food groups here, sugar, preservatives. You know, of course guys . . . " and off he rambled.

Google-eyed, the other climbers and hikers nudged each other and looked depreciatingly at their meager handfuls of lunch and back to Frank. Meanwhile, he had unwrapped the ham and carved off a large piece for his sandwich.

"Man, this is eatin'!" Out came a much folded, wrinkled and smeared *NY Times Book Review*. He sat down and happily turned the pages.

"Jesus!" Pete complained under his breath for the hundredth time. "Everything but the kitchen sink!" Only this time, he sounded genuinely envious.

Night of the Laughing Dead

By: John Arrington

No shit! There I was, flat on my back at 3,984 feet. I was dying.
Blue spots swam before my eyes. Each new seizure made me roll
from side to side and gasp. I pounded my fists into the soft foam
mattress. I couldn't see out over the tops of my cheeks or make
sounds other than feeble gurgles. Breathing? Forget breathing.
Breathing was entirely out of the question. I was ferchrissakes
dying...right there in the back of my pickup twenty feet from
where my new girlfriend was trying to take her first whiz in the
woods. Honest, I tried not to laugh. I tried desperately not to laugh.
Trying not to laugh only made it hurt worse.

We were car camping. Yeah, I know, car camping is for Wusses,
but Christina is more of a city girl than a mountain momma. I
wanted her introduction to the outdoors to be gentle and enjoyable.
I mean, I prefer doing switch-backs with at least 85 pounds on my
back and sleeping on a pointy rock, but when you're in love you
have to make sacrifices.

Campsite #129, on the C Loop, consisted of an asphalt parking
patch, a picnic table chained to a cement anchor, a fire ring, a water
faucet, and an electrical outlet. Ahhhhh, wilderness! There were

some plastic garbage cans and recycling bins down by the entrance where we'd paid ten bucks to spend the night. Ahhhhh, rip-off! An asphalt "trail" led from #129 to a brick facility about a hundred yards away. It had hot showers, surprisingly clean toilets and a place to wash your dishes. It wasn't quite the same as pitching a VE-24 in a hanging valley with a killer view, but in general, not a bad place to spend the night. Hey, we had trees, pine-scented air, chipmunks stealing our food, and a nice view of the mountains out beyond the first ridge of Winnebuggers.

Winnebuggers?

Motor homes, dude! We were surrounded. I'm talkin' 65-footers, with all the good stuff like satellite dishes and bass boats and air conditioners up on top, and dirt bikes and folded up aluminum lawn furniture strapped across the back, and a rusty Huffy 10-Speed lashed to the front bumper and a Toyota 4X4 in tow. I was in one once. They had a microwave oven and a TV and a shower and a ferchrissakes vibrating king-sized bed. No shit! It vibrated. I swear to God!

My pickup has a leaky camper shell, an old foam mattress, and about 40 pounds of yellow lab fur stuck to everything!

Anyway... we'd driven all the way from Boise. We were tired and hungry and ready to kick back and enjoy the great out-of-doors. I loaded the barbecue up with charcoal, squirted it with about half a can of lighter fluid and tossed in the match! In a few minutes the coals were glowing and the chicken breasts were sizzling on the grill. While we waited, Christina got a lesson in MSR stove lighting, Swiss Army knife can opener technique, and the intricacies of heating up a can of S&W Texas Style Barbecue Beans in a battered old Sigg pot. She did a great job, but I burnt the hell out of the chicken.

"Smoke keeps the mosquitoes away," I alibied.

The smoke screen was truly awesome. We could hear Winnebugger doors slamming and windows closing and old farts cursing. The Camp Host dropped by and asked if everything was all right.

"Well, it is if you like extra crispy," I said sheepishly.

The "host" was not amused. He asked us, and we solemnly promised, not to set the forest on fire or cause any more... uhh... disturbances.

By the time we finished eating, the sun was setting and it was getting awfully damned cold. We crawled in the back of the truck to see if a half-pint of brandy, a bag of Oreos, four comforters and some serious scroon would warm us up. They did! Afterwards we cuddled under the mountain of comforters until she said, "I have to pee."

"Well?"

"It's cold out there. I'll freeze before I get to the bathrooms. Do you think they're heated?"

"Awww, just go out behind the truck."

"You mean, just go outside and . . . pee? What if someone sees me?"

"No one's gonna see you. They're all watching Lawrence Welk reruns. Just be quiet. They'll never know you're out there."

She considered the options, gave me a quick kiss and quietly lowered the tailgate. I wondered if I'd be able to hear her pee. I was still turned on from the sex and the thought of listening to her was having a powerful effect on me. Suddenly, I was intensely interested in what was about to take place. I held my breath. It was so quiet I could hear my digital watch ticking. Then I heard the unmistakable sound of a descending zipper.

That's when it happened. That's when the intense stillness and my erotic reverie was shattered by a sound unlike any I'd ever heard. That's when all hell broke loose. It began as a nearly silent whooshing sound and quickly built into a crescendo of staggering proportions.

Whoosh . . . f oosh . . . fuf . . . Fuf . . . FFFAAAAAAARRRRRTTTT!

Honest, I tried not to laugh. I tried desperately not to laugh. But how could I not laugh? This was no ordinary, polite, little girl fart. It was the ferchrissakes fart of the century! Not since the eruption of Mt. Saint Helens had the Pacific Northwest been subjected to anything like it. The ground trembled. Shock waves slammed into the side of the truck. Pine cones fell like hail stones in a Kansas storm. A tsunami ripped across Crater Lake. Big Foot cowered in his lair! Lights came on in all the motor homes. The camp host came running with a fire extinguisher and one of those Maglites™

with about a hunnert D Cells inside. Do those things turn night into day or what?

And, there, in the middle of all this commotion was my sweetie, squatting in the fire ring, laughing hysterically, trousers around her ankles, buns covered with soot, and frantically trying not to pee all over herself.

Ten people died that night. No Shit! It was the night of the laughing dead.

1. Remember when a Motel Six cost six bucks a night?

2. If you have amorous aspirations when car camping, try comforters instead of sleeping bags. They provide plenty of warmth and much more freedom of movement.

Don Jesus

By: John Long

Through rags of shifting clouds we caught glimpses of a great cascade plunging past an orange wall and fusing into a billowing bridal veil at the boulder-strewn base, 3,212 feet below: Angel Falls, the world's largest. In two days, for network television cameras, Jim Bridwell and I were to rappel down the rock wall just next to the gusher. The assignment looked different than I'd imagined back in Los Angeles.

The creaky D9 transport plane rattled into a thundershower, but quickly burst free into clear airspace. To the left and to the right, before and behind, rolling, mounting, sinking, rising, like huge swells in a huge green sea, was the Venezuelan rain forest. Shortly, we skimmed over a copper lake, jounced along a lumpy dirt airstrip and deplaned in Canaima, waving through curtains of flying ants that follow every rain.

Canaima was no "jungle resort," rather a smattering of rustic cabins, a small cafeteria and a gigantic, open air bar on the shore of the lake. And Indians. Pamon Indians. Short and bronzed, with guarded, feral eyes, they ran the place—cooked the food, cleaned the rooms, kept the books.

According to Baltazar, a production manager based in Caracas, Pamons had lived around the lake for centuries, and their position in the heart of the rain forest was so remote that they hadn't encountered outsiders until shortly after World War II. Diamonds were found on surrounding rock outcrops, and soon thereafter, every able-bodied Pamon male was sweating his breechcloth off at three flourishing mines. A few Pamon elders, however, played a more crucial role than mere laborers.

Over the eons, the Pamons had developed systematic rituals to interpret the tempestuous elements. Their very survival depended on it, for one glance at Canaima's rotting, proliferating, monstrously exaggerated botany and you'd understand how a small seed, planted in the fecund peat, could swell to a three-kilo melon in a matter of weeks; and conversely, how a relentless monsoon could flood the entire village in a matter of hours. It followed that the antique art of divining storms would be used to the diamond miners' advantage; and there are stories still told of how the mines were constructed and worked in spurts between tortuous rains, as foretold by Pamon shaman.

The mines are played out now, and monsoonproof cinderblock and steel dwellings have long replaced the poetic reed huts. Grandsons of the old shamans are presently turned out in pressed Levis and Ray Bans, dancing to "Las Chicas del Can" in the bar. As far as we could tell, time and "progress" had completely severed the charmed alliance these people once had with their milieu.

The next morning Jim and I helicoptered back up to the falls to scout things. Following a ten-minute downpour, we were dismayed to see the gusher surge threefold almost instantly, a perfect torrent plunging down our proposed line of descent, just right of the main waterfall. Back in Canaima we asked Baltazar about weather reports. He laughed. They didn't even have a shortwave radio in Canaima. But there was another fascinating option—Don Jesus, the last savant of the old knowledge. We sighed, but Baltazar insisted that while the shaman was a relic even amongst his own people, the pilots (flying by the seat of their pantolones, with no hard info about the surrounding weather save for what they could see) listened to the old man closely indeed because Don Jesus could "read the rain," or so swore Baltazar.

"Why not?" Jim said. We gave Baltazar twenty Bolivars (roughly five dollars) for Don Jesus' fee, and a little mestizo boy took the money and set off for the Indian's hut. I figured if nothing else, the old man's prediction would have decades of local living behind it.

Shortly, the kid returned, and Jim and I followed him down a dark muddy path that rambled along the margin of the copper lake. The trail veered into the bush to a medley of bamboo and rattan huts. We stopped at the biggest one. Clusters of heliotrope hung in festoons from old tires by the open door, and a screeching spider monkey, tethered to a rusted tractor rim, nearly choked itself trying to get at Jim. We ducked inside.

Don Jesus was a lanky, pulled-out specimen with a face like Methuselah's grandfather—weathered, serene, religious. There was no flesh to the man; we could see the working of his bones, and his eyes were dark and grave. He sat on a small stool, we on the reed floor. Aside from a sputtering Coleman lantern and a portrait of La Virgin del Coromoto hanging on the wall, the hut was empty.

I explained in Spanish that tomorrow we had to go down Angel Falls on a big rope, that it would take many dangerous hours to do so, and if it rained too much, the falls could swell and possibly drown us. We really needed to know about tomorrow's skies.

I was surprised that I could squat there in a bamboo hut in central nowhere, asking a withered old Indian to divine the weather for us—and really mean it. But the presence of the man, solemn and steady as Father Time, brought a certain greatness to the scene, and seemed to hurl us back to an age when simple questions had simple answers, and when an entire culture hung in the balance with the precision of these answers.

Don Jesus nodded toward a wide leaf at his feet upon which lay a small mound of whitish powder—chopo, a plant mixture said to be fatal to a common man and to drive dogs mad. The young mestizo scooped a tiny portion into the end of a three-foot bamboo shaft. Don Jesus held the business end to his nose; the kid inhaled and blew the dose up the shaft and deep into Don Jesus. He slouched back, tears streaming down his face, his eyes waxing to infinity. Slowly, he slipped into a sort of waking dream, and took up a small wooden sleeve, elaborately carved and smudged by generations of hands and smoke.

With a flick of the wrist, he tossed out several straight twigs, and for some minutes studied their position on the floor. Only later would I be told that this first toss concerned spacial matters:

somewhere in that tangle of twigs was Angel Falls. The second toss involved the weather, which he divined in seconds. The third toss, which he lingered over with stony enchantment, concerned time: when would the clouds break? The last toss concerned our suerte, or luck.

Throughout, I was struck not by a sense of black artifice or native hooey, rather how natural the whole business seemed. The old man had thrown those sticks into an intermediate zone where chance and fact converged. Somewhere, traced in the shadow of those sticks, lay our future, plain as water—if you were on speaking terms with sun and sky and God. Four tosses, four modalities intertwined tight as the reed walls. Nothing strange about it.

Since the chopo, it seemed as though his spirit, abandoning his body, had wandered to far away places; but when he looked up, Don Jesus was right back with the living again.

"If you hurry tomorrow, you should be fine," he said. "But any delay and things will turn grave."

"How grave?" I asked.

"That depends on your luck," he said, smiling slightly. And the mestizo kid led us away.

By seven the next morning, Jim and I had thrown a rope over the brink of the world's largest waterfall and were ready to hurry down. But by the time dozens of cameramen were helicoptered into position, it was early afternoon and the skies were slate grey and snarling. An hour later, after we had rappelled 1,000 feet, the clouds cut loose. The falls swelled and washed over us like a glacial blast. Had a harsh wind not blown the gusher away from us, we might still be hanging on that rope. Four hours after starting, we finally touched down—soaked, freezing, covered in green slime, and played all the way out—and dove into the last copter heading south. We spent two hours grinding through fog and thunder and jet-black night. We got lost. Twice. When we finally clanked into Canaima we were running on fumes and slammed down on to the helipad so hard we broke a skid.

Later that night, as the fifty-man production crew danced to El Tigre El Magnifico and swilled bottle after bottle of raw cane liquor, I made my way back to Don Jesus' hut and told him what had happened. As the old shaman nodded his head slightly and gently fingered the carved wooden sleeve, I had the exhilarating feeling that I'd taken a ride on that funky velvet chair in H.G. Wells' Time Machine, and was again part of something strange and wonderful and old as rain itself.

"I told you to hurry," Don Jesus finally said, "because it is easier to walk the dry path than the muddy one. But it did not matter so much because the sticks told me you were lucky."

Playing in the Mud

By: Fred and Gloria Jones

One of our greatest joys during the years we lived in northern Virginia was playing in the mud of the marshes inside the barrier islands of the Atlantic coast. We escaped the work week in Washington, D.C. by fleeing to the shore, tossing our car-top tin boat into one of the many rivers and exploring the byways of the marshes.

Blue crabs, those delectable morsels, were there to be gathered and we worked hard at it. Hard-shelled clams lay just under the surface of the mud and could most easily be found by walking barefoot and pulling the boat along. They (the clams) feel like a rock under foot. This particular clam-finding technique is fine, until you step on a crab and it reaches around your foot with its needle-pointed claws and pinches real hard!

A favorite area for us was Folly Creek, snaking its way through marshes out to Metomkin Island and into the ocean. When flounder, sea trout or croakers were running, we'd anchor over a hole in the creek and do our best to fill the boat. Black skimmers were always working the creek, scooting along with their big, red lower bills dragging through the water to snare a minnow. On contact, the head jerks down, then is jerked up and the fish swallowed. For blind trolling, the skimmers do very well.

On this particular occasion, we were poking our way up a channel we had not been in before, feeling every inch of the way like the mother lode of clams lay around the next bend. When our little 10-hp Evinrude touched bottom, we jumped out and pulled the boat up the shallowing channel. It was low tide and pretty soon we ran out of water. My wife Gloria and our son John began exploring the exposed mud flats while I fiddled with the boat.

The mud was soft and Gloria stepped into a particularly juicy spot that grabbed on to her waders real tight. John slogged over to help. He got alongside, grabbed the top of her waders and gave a huge yank. This did two things—one, it ripped her waders, and two, it pulled him in deeper while she stayed put.

By this time there was enough commotion to penetrate the fog of my concentration to the fact that the boat was no longer sitting in the mud—it was floating just the teeniest bit. At last—the tide was coming back in—we could move on up the channel with ease and find that great mother lode of tasty comestibles! But, wait! Two of the party were yelling that they were stuck in the mud! How inconvenient—just when things were looking up.

But wait, again! Gloria and John were now buried up to their waists and the water was creeping toward them. There wasn't going to be much time to figure how to unstick them. The first reaction of rushing right over to pull them out seemed to be a good prescription for having a threesome waiting in close family unity for the water to arrive, rise to fill the waders, bathe the armpits, tickle the chin and so forth. After an indecent interval of thrashing about, screaming and hollering, the crabs would have a great banquet and three more names would go down in the local annals of dumb-ass city slickers.

Casting about for a board or some device to poke towards them for support on the mud, my frantic mind finally focused on ... the tin boat.

Of course, how simple! Merely tow it over and ... no, how about pushing it over. That's a smart boy. Push it over the nice, wet, slippery mud ... careful! Don't bang it into Gloria! Whoops, sorry honey. Climb over the transom ... damn motor anyway! Walk forward, reach over the side, hook under Gloria's armpits and heave... and heave... and heave. Sounding like an elephant pulling its great foot out of the mud, here rose the creature from the Black Lagoon—all over with mud in the nice clean boat. Then, more heaves to collect creature number two and there we were, a family reunited. And feeling pretty good about it, too, as the rising water floated the boat and drifted us off to wherever it wanted. We were too busy hugging each other and getting all muddy together to really care.

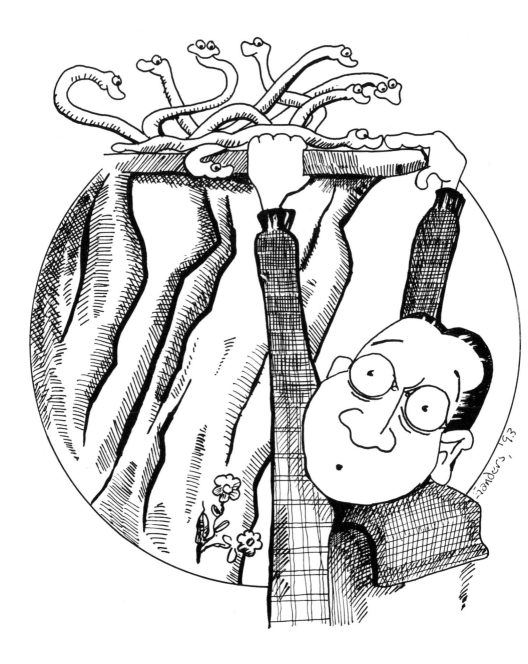

Holy Batman! It's Raining Snakes

By: Gary Catt

I had eyeballed the rocky outcropping often from a couple of different angles. I had hiked the ridge above it and skinny-dipped in the brook below it. Although it required a lot less savvy than a technical climb, it looked somewhat challenging—presenting a diversion on a summer day hike with my buddy Yoblow (a nick-name earned for things that should never be explained in print).

The climb was going pretty easy. The morning had been cool, but now the sun was beating down on our backs, warming the rock face to the touch.

I more or less followed behind, mirroring Yoblow's moves. Yoblow worked his way to a slight overhang. He was standing in a foot-wide toehold, arms fully extended over his head, fingers lapped over a ledge.

"I'm going to pull up onto the ledge," he announced.

I watched him lift straight up about ten inches and then freeze. Here I'd like to say he screamed like hell, but he didn't. He

squeaked. Something like "aaheeeek!" Then he dropped back to
the toehold, face pressed flush to the wall, his hands still lapped
over the ledge, arms stretched full length above his head.

"Aaheeeek!" he squeaked again.

"What's up?" I asked.

"Snakes. Lots of f-----g snakes," he whispered. "I pulled up, just
got my eyes over the edge and there they were . . . all looking at me.
I think they're copperheads."

There was a lot of stress in Yoblow's voice. And, hell, I don't
like snakes all that much. I suggested a hasty retreat.

Yoblow, however, was frozen in place—fully extended, his fingers still rolled over the top of the overhang.

"I'm afraid to move," he whispered. "It's my fingers. If I move
'em, they'll look like mice and the snakes will strike. I can feel one
moving over my fingers now."

Yoblow's voice began to stretch a bit there. Fortunately, snakes
can't hear.

"Why don't you just pull both hands down at one time, real
quick like," I offered.

"It won't work, the snakes will get pulled down on my head."

"Well, you can just stand there then. I'll go down and get my
snakebite kit." Jeeze, somebody had to be rational about this.

When I got back, Yoblow was starting to weaken.

"I think it shit on my fingers," he moaned.

This struck me as unusual. I, for one, had never seen a snake
shit, although I've come to know people on occasion who could fit
the description.

"Well, you've got to get your hands down," I told him. "I've got
the snakebite kit, so just yank 'em out."

Then it struck me. What we needed was a diversion. I would lob
a big rock up onto the ledge and at the same time, Yoblow would
yank his hands out. Great idea.

Yoblow agreed.

I grabbed a good five-pound chunk of limestone and lobbed it up
over the edge.

Suddenly, it was raining snakes. Snakes falling from the sky. Little ones. Big ones. Wounded ones. It took me a second to realize it,

but the snakes were behaving like lemmings, squiggling one after another off the ledge and plunging downward around us.

In the chaos, Yoblow yanked his hands off the ledge and pressed himself into the rock face trying to Rushmorize himself. We both escaped unscathed as the snakes hit the rocks below our feet and slithered from sight.

Yoblow and I worked a wide path downward around where all of the snakes had landed.

In the truck on the way home, I told him, "I don't own a snake-bite kit."

The Long Road to Cokeville

By: Jody Foss

Wyoming breeds mosquitoes at an alarming rate along the irrigation ditches. The road to Cokeville was paved with mosquitoes; I had shorts on most of the way and the annoying little insects fed on my legs. They are hard on me especially, since I have a bet going with David, and cannot wear any repellent.

"I promise you, Jod," he said to me right before we headed back to Park City, "if you don't wear repellent, pretty soon you will be immune to them. You won't taste good to them any more."

"How long will it take?" I asked him. "The length of the trail?"

He laughed. So far I wish I never would have made this bet with him. I don't think he realized how many mosquitoes there really are out here. Debbie has some of this surplus bug stuff from Viet Nam, and uses it like perfume. They seem to leave her alone.

I got off to open a gate and they zeroed in on the tender pinkness of my calves, particularly enjoying the back of the knee. My legs were covered with mosquitoes.

"I wish my jeans weren't packed away on the mule," I whined to Debbie.

It was torture today; long, hot, and miserable. My legs were welted solidly from the top of my gray wool socks to the bottom of my green shorts, and a little beyond.

We were fifteen miles south of Cokeville, heading up the irrigation ditch on a perfectly graded dirt road.

"Just a second, Cowboy," I said to my horse. "I need to tighten your cinch. This saddle is about to fall off." I could feel it was very loose, so I lowered myself carefully to the ground. I could instantly hear the buzz of mosquitoes rise to a crescendo, in a feeding frenzy, as they headed for prime positions; the best my thighs and calves had to offer. Their favorite place to dine was the tender inside of my thigh, right below the line of my shorts. I tried to stay calm, but I was about ready to blow.

To make things worse, Deb and John had ridden ahead of me, and were by this time almost out of sight, on top of a little rise on the road about a quarter of a mile ahead. Nothing a horse hates more than to lag behind the herd. To say the least, Cowboy was more than a little excited about it. My dog Robin circled us nervously; she also was not interested in losing the mule who carried her dinner.

"Easy, Boy," I said to him, as I loosened his cinch before retightening it. He watched the top of the bluff carefully, his big, brown ears pointing earnestly towards the horizon, intent on his herd, as Comanche and the other animals disappeared from view. This was not something he liked; in fact it was the one thing, besides the rustling of raincoats and tarps, that made the spotted horse very anxious.

Unfortunately, in that same moment, a yellow jacket landed on Cowboy's belly. I saw the insect land, half a second before my horse exploded, leaping straight up in the air, about four feet off the ground; straight up, like the Roadrunner, his legs a blur of movement as they formed a wheel under him. I blinked and he was gone, bucking insanely down the road, through the sage; legs flying back behind him, kicking, jumping, trying to lose the yellow jacket and the saddle. I watched as my meager household shot off his sides, as he kicked out his legs with such force he truly looked like a cartoon horse. His only concern now was to catch up with Comanche and the others.

I fell backward voluntarily into the sandy soil between two sage bushes and watched as Cowboy became a tiny dot on the horizon, then disappeared out of sight. I sat there laughing, silently, then got up, dusted myself off, and began walking stiffly down the road. Robin was laughing at me, as only a dog can, with her big pink tongue reaching out for the canteen. Just as she realized that the canteen had disappeared over the ridge, along with everything else, she looked at me with sincere Labrador concern, urging me along through the sage, in the direction of my itinerant band. I knew that Cowboy had caught up with Deb and John and the pack train. I hoped they had caught him and were up ahead waiting for me.

I found my saddle bags first; thrown off the side of the road into the middle of a sage brush. They were empty. My saddle had come off around his tail and back legs, because the cinch was still fastened together. I smiled, picturing him wriggling out of the saddle.

"There's my address book, Rob," I said to my dog, who was nosing her way from page to page of my address book, finding the A's and then the B's and so on, up the dirt road to Cokeville. I found my canteen and sat down in the sage.

"Here, girl, here Rob, have a little drink, your tongue's getting pretty long!" She gracefully trotted towards me, dropping the M page of the address book at my feet. "Thanks girl." I cupped my hands and she licked at the water very slowly and carefully, so she didn't lose any. There was my toothbrush and toothpaste, in a plastic bag, in the barrow ditch. Then I came across my hairbrush, my tape recorder—seemingly unharmed—and my notebook, all in the same big bush. Flung there, then suspended, hanging on the stiff branches of the aromatic sage.

I picked up the rest of my belongings off the road: the lucky horseshoe I had carried in my saddle bag since the High Uintas, a red bandanna, some Band Aids, a Chap Stick, skin cream, three pens, some hydrogen peroxide, some gauze, sunglasses, letters I had received in Evanston, and a little bag of rubber bands and leather ties that almost escaped my eye—pitched under a sage brush. I walked along, fairly confident that I had everything, and strode the rest of the way at a good clip with my saddle over one shoulder and my saddle bags over the other.

"How does Cowboy carry this thing?" I wondered aloud to Robin.

We caught up with Deb and John a mile later, just enough time to work the crink out of my legs. They were eating peanut butter sandwiches and dried fruit by the time I caught up with them. Sarah Jane, and the horses, including my spirited Cowboy, were tied to fence posts.

"Boy, Jod, I'll tell you what," Deb said to me through a mouth stuffed full of fluffy wheat bread and peanut butter. "That horse was flying when he caught up to us! He didn't slow down until he was head to head with Sarah Jane. I swear, the boy's in love!"

I put out my hand and pouted, begging for a sandwich, then dropped to my knees and really begged until John threw me a dried pear. It tasted better than anything I have tasted in a long time. I savored the sweet, chewy fruit and looked at Deb, not saying a word. It would take a while to live this one down. After a half hour or so, I packed up Cowboy, tightened his cinch, and we headed off towards Cokeville.

The Tai Chi
of the
Critical Moment

By: Paul McHugh

Ever seen a dog with a pure jones for running as he finally gets taken out, his leash is unsnapped, then he sprints free and wild down a beach?

Recall the shining eyes, the lolling tongue, the tiny sand cascades from paws digging deep for traction on a high-torque turn, the deliriously joyful barks, the breeze that ripples the red-bronze fur, the wetblack nose rooting with eager frenzy through heaps of seaweed, flotsam and wrack . . . but the dog abandons it on a whim to wheel directly into splashing runs out through wave spray, followed by teasing escapes from a tug of undertow and backwash of surf?

Riding a motorcycle is like that.

You see, this joyous sense of play, this pure delight in motion is part of the fuel of the physical animal, and part of our birthright as well. Motorcycles so amp our senses that we are reached in deeper places, and inspired to thrust our minds into more captivating sensual levels than those strata which we ordinarily so fussily and fretfully manage.

In such shining instants, our inner animal is seduced to leap forth and dance through our skins. But much more than the rapture of a playing animal makes itself manifest when grave and proximate danger is added to the summons.

As a dog rides in the bed of a pick-up, his experience is amped by the power of the machinery, and each major sense is stimulated to the maximum. His nose is jammed with a stream of odors both subtle and strong, his eyes filled with a blur of passing landscape, his ears tune into a symphony borne to him through undulating white noise of the slipstream wind.

By contrast, most human drivers of automobiles remain well-insulated from the world through which they pass. Manufacturers may hype a certain hot model's handling, but primarily, a modern car is created to isolate you from the landscape. There's cushy suspension to homogenize the surface of the terrain, stereophonic laser disc players to mask its sounds, plus an air-conditioner capable of wiping out any ambient climate.

On a motorcycle, you're more like the dog in the pick-up. The warmth of each ridge, the coolth of every dell wrap about you immediately as you wend through them. The fragrance of each earthen bank, dank willow-clad creek, or field of wildflowers washes around and up under your helmet only to be instantly replaced by the new bouquet of odors awaiting you around the curve . . . which may just happen to include a freshly squished skunk — PHee-YEW!!

And visuals sharp and crystal clear rush toward you from straight-on, blur to abstract streaks in your peripheral vision, then take real shape again briefly in the rear view mirrors shortly before they vanish forever. This is the 360-degree movie through which you fly . . .

A thin shriek of wind whistles past your helmet, the bass thrum of the big engine vibrates right up through the seat into your spine, as do a hum and mumble of the tires on the pavement. Part and parcel of this sensory stream is a gamut of logistical meaning that's speedily weighed by the brain, then fed flowing back through the body in the opposite direction, rushing back out through the nerves of your feet and fingers as a continuous stream of operating commands to the big mechanical beast humming between your legs.

You grab just the right amount of rpm's with a throttle twist from your right fist so the beast drops onto a power surge at just the precise spot, so you can snap open your left fingers just as if your clutch lever was a bowstring, and you yourself become the arrow that darts straight out from the nadir of that curve in the swale.

In such a fashion, you not only grow to appreciate undulations of the terrain in a manner known mostly to low-flying goshawks, you also feel a telepathic communion with a road engineer, that very one who designed this sinuous sequence of banked curves which permits you to swoop and recoup your carefully invested momentum instead of having to jerk it around or chop it roughly back with your brakes. And you wonder if somewhere back in that engineer's mind way back then there wasn't the germ of this thought, "Ah, this road of mine is one smooth and beautiful sumbitch, it'll be pure delight for someone to charge out snake it up on a big roaring chopper some crisp fall day."

It is an ultimate sensation to shape all that information rushing into and out of you, so that your mind, the terrain and the beast all unite in the experience, and the motorcycle is raised like Frankenstein's monster into near sentience and obvious animation by the kiss of your pleasure in its movement.

But all of that experience, and all that conditioning and pleasure pale in comparison beside the forces that emerge when one is forced to put all one knows, and more than all one knows, to a test, a test in which matters of life and death must be decided in an instant.

Here's the scene: a crisp autumn night in Tallahassee, Florida, in 1971.

It's about 1 a.m., and I'm riding a black Triumph Bonneville motorcycle back from an evening of wine, cheese and literary blather at a college professor's home.

Now this "Trumpet" — our slang term for Triumph bikes back then — was one hot putt. It had been a track racer, reconverted for street use, and its 650cc vertical twin engine packed a potent 210 pounds of compression in both cylinders. So I'm cruising down Monroe St. to the major intersection in town and yeah, I'm ballin' that jack at maybe twice the speed limit. Hey, I'm young, and there's few cops around at that early A.M. hour, and those shortie exhaust pipes I had on emitted a burbling roar that I loved to hear reverberate back off those big storefront windows as they rattled in their frames.

Those big bikes had a bass toot that stimulated every major gland in a teenager's body. Could be, that's why we called 'em Trumpets.

As I rumble blithely up the low hill where Tallahassee's two major highways cross under a traffic light, suddenly my mildly ecstatic, high-speed cruise turns into an invitation to die.

This turkey coming the other way in a red sportscar just cranks a left turn right in front of me.

That's bad.

Next, he sees me coming, freaks out, hits his brakes and stops. Sideways, and blocking the road. Dead in front of me.

That's real bad. "Oh Fuck," are two words that spring to mind.

Amazing how your mind just shoots right into hyperspace when something like that occurs. Time itself seems to slow down. An astounding number of perceptions and choices and moves seems to fill the silences between heartbeats.

OK. No room to swerve. Gotta bring the speed down as much as possible before impact. Crank down hard on those mushy Triumph brakes! Oops. Rear wheel's locking up and the back end of the bike is sliding around past the freewheeling front end. Balance is fragile and dicey. Don't want to lay the motorcycle down because then I'll go under that low sportscar and probably get his transmission embedded in my cerebrum.

If I'm absolutely gonna hit it, I'd rather be riding high and have the chance to launch my body up and over the car.

But sliding the Trumpet in this crazy sideways screeching posture ain't something I can handle for more than a microsecond! But wait—my mind goes plunging like a wildman through a haystack of solutions in a crazed search for that one straw that might possibly be turned into a magic wand—I suddenly and luridly recalled a scene from a movie I'd just seen, a documentary of motorcycle riding called "On Any Sunday," with some cameo scenes in it by actor Steve McQueen. There had also been some scenes of flat-track racing that showed guys going into broadslides on dirt curves, then slowing down without brakes as they steered by goosing the throttle.

Seemed like a real good idea to pull off a broadslide now.

I'd never done anything even remotely like it before.

But necessity can be a mother.

So, let's just assume I can do it.

Keep the rear tire sliding now, bozo, keep the front tire rolling so you can steer, use rear brake pressure to keep the rear tire where you want it, keep your balance on the foot pegs, and Hey! ain't this something?

Now you're broadsliding!

My tires and front brake drum are screeching, doom is still rapidly approaching, and my emotional state can be summarized as terrified. But somewhere in my brain I am also smiling: God bless those limey bike builders. They may have made Trumpets with the crummiest electrics since Benjamin Franklin's kite string, and scumbag carburetors that are impossible to tune, but man, the sweet-handling of this frame geometry on this here motorcycle is an ergonomic marvel.

As disastrous as the overall situation is, something about my barely balanced, skittering slide across pavement towards that sportscar feels just, absolutely perfect.

However, goddammit, although this broadslide lets me slow without putting the bike right smack down into a medley of grinding metal on the pavement, my situation is only marginally improved. Now, it looks like I'll just crash into that sportscar with the right side of my body, instead of head-on.

It does not seem as though this shift in my circumstances really constitutes a significant improvement.

But that distracting thought is immediately swatted out of my mind by a much larger concern. How can I possibly get out of THIS part of the fix?

Well, why not shoot the moon!

I WAS able to assume that I could broadslide.

Now, let's assume I'm psychic.

Thus, I can broadcast a special, mental message to the driver of the sportscar, with the force of a billion candlepower lighthouse lamp lens that beams into his grey and swirling foggy mental fog with a dense and swiftly transmitted ditty that goes something like this:

HEY THERE STUPID, THE BEST WAY FOR THREE HUN-DRED POUNDS OF BRITISH STEEL TO NOT WIND UP IN YOUR LAP BY WAY OF CAROMING OFF YOUR GIRL-FRIEND'S FACE WHO SITS NOW BESIDE YOU IN THE FRONT SEAT WITH HER JAW HANGING DOWN TO HER BELLYBUTTON IS IF YOU TAKE YOUR GOLDDANG FOOT OFF THE BRAKE PEDAL, PUT IT ON THE ACCELERATOR, AND CHUG ON OUT OF MY WAY!!!

And I'll be darned if he didn't respond.

He did just as I'd instructed him.

But he did it with agonizing, heart-wrenching slowness. Or was my sense of his forward motion only relative to the awesome speed of neurons firing and synapses snapping in my brain as my body's internal tachometer soared past redline? Had I entered into some surreal state of overdrive, where thoughts and impressions and choices whirled through my consciousness with a speed that would make a tornado look like a zephyr?

Perhaps even the second sweep of a wall clock would look to me now as if it was groaning, staggering, taking an eternity to swing from one second hatch mark on the clock face to the next.

In any case, even though he was now moving, I foresaw I'd still mightily crash into his rear bumper unless I could somehow turn this broadsliding sled back into a rolling motorcycle and swiftly swerve around him.

So. Right now. How do I get out of this friggin' broadslide?

Again, the mind leaped.

I take no personal credit for this, by the way. Whatever it was happening within me was as outlandish as stumbling onto the dance floor behind your new girlfriend in dread of your very first major junior high school social embarrassment and suddenly discovering you'd been demonically—but magically—possessed by the ghost of Fred Astaire.

This time, the mind leaped into a dark sea of unconscious intuition gradually accumulated from the past six years of riding motorcycles on everything from sand and gravel to wet pavement. How do you get out of a broadslide? The answer seemed to resonate right up out of my nerves. Take your foot off the brake, unlock the rear wheel, and goose the throttle. The envisioned sweetness of the move just seemed right. It harmonized with the situation.

And there were no more milliseconds left for a second guess.

I twisted that throttle grip like I was turning the doorknob on the portal to my personal future, and the Trumpet swerved back into a straight line of travel as the squeal of the rear tire was supplanted by the motor's roar. And so my body and that motorcycle whipped around the rear bumper of that still slowly moving sportscar with nary a centimeter of space to spare.

Then I pulled to the curb, switched off the bike, took a breath that seemed like the first deep breath I'd had in weeks, and sat there shaking. My pulse hammered so furiously, it felt as if it was about to blow my forehead off. Shadows and streetlights seemed to shift and waver in color as my perception of time wound gradually back down to normal level, and it was like I could feel the hum of a dynamo fading down to its ordinary rpm.

Very, very carefully, I restarted the bike and drove home. But lying awake that night — and for years since then — I pondered the remarkable, magical transformation that had occurred. That spontaneous and wondrous shift in my time sense, perceptions and reactions during those few heartbeats when my life had seemed at risk. It had seemed that at every fast-paced critical juncture there had been a path laid out in my mind with the absolute lucidity of a neon arrow glittering in the void. All that had been required to survive was the boldness to choose and commit instantly to that path.

To mint some words and coin a phrase: let's call this transformation The Tai Chi of the Critical Moment.

To experience this high-speed transmogrification is our birthright.

Man — and Woman — the animals — come equipped with the biochemical gear to take on a sabertooth. To experience that transformation in all its hair-raising glory is to discover something important about our identity. It is to plunge our bucket into a well-spring of innate power.

One blessing and curse of human affairs in the very late 20th century is that we barely allow ourselves to experience just an overture to that powerful and ancient reflex. But involving our bodies in "risk sports" not only permits a reconnect to the vibrancy of our animal nature, it also allows a complete, physical follow-through to a conclusion.

One makes tremendous discoveries in that process.

My friend, mountaineering writer Eric Perlman, has said: "High-risk sports are mentally and physically addictive. Forget cocaine and LSD — those are just synthetic triggers that send the real drugs into action. When an avalanche rakes the climbing route, or the kayak flips in a gnarly hole, every eye-opening, pain-killing drug in your body rips through the nervous system like a Chinese fire drill.

"Muscle fibers fire faster. Emotions hit warp speed. Thoughts kick into hyperdrive. The higher the risk, the hotter the dose. Adrenaline, epinephrine, endorphins, dynorphins and dozens of others — those are the pure stuff that money can't buy."

Perlman is right about the delicious intensity of this hormonal cocktail. When the hormone-amped body presents its possible moves to the crisis-focused mind, life becomes absolutely dazzling in its clarity and vigor; and awareness becomes simultaneously sweeping and sharp.

Tai Chi refers to an old Chinese martial art, and the Chi that is summoned and nourished is the essential life force. To feel it erupt and dominate decisively a critical moment is not only to be exhilarated, but to be informed in no uncertain terms who we are at our core. It gives us a hint of the sort of talents we might unlock if we could only pay more attention to them.

I quit riding motorcycles. I grew entirely too sensitive to their dangers to continue. Besides, I had taken up whitewater kayaking, and I told myself, "A man doesn't need TWO things like this. Only so much luck to go around!"

Then in 1989, after nine years of doing without, I bought a BMW R100GS, and began again. I had come to realize that it wasn't only moments of high crisis that had energized my nerves.

A steady growth of awareness had once come to me from just riding around on bikes. What had made me such a conscious and defensive driver nowadays was the motorcycle experience in toto. Constant exposure to risk had rubbed the nerves ripe and ready, whenever I was on the road. Constant work on processing rogue variables had made me program in a response to always look for escape routes far in advance of need.

When riding a motorcycle, your own skills and abilities are also among the things that should never be taken for granted. Even apparent constants—the adhesion of your tires to the road surface—will not remain the same. A patch of oil, a streak of mud, or an unanticipated need to hit the brakes can suddenly turn your magic carpet into a tumbling bucket of bolts.

Of course, that unpredictability permeates all the rest of life. But riding a motorcycle makes it obvious.

I guess the key argument that swung me back into the doggone beautiful world of big putts was something I heard from a biker who had never taken a break from the sport. For a newspaper story on motorcycling, I was interviewing Dennis Casey, who rode on weekends, and worked the rest of the time as a carpenter in the East Bay. When I learned he'd ridden steadily for the past 20 years, I wondered why the inherent dangers hadn't slowed him down or stopped him, in the name of all the presumed responsibilities of adult life.

"Sure," Casey said on the phone. "Bikes are dangerous. But, you know, another school of thought goes, you could step out your door tomorrow, stroll down the sidewalk and still get hit by a truck.

"So, my idea is when death comes to you, you might as well be doing what the hell turns you on. Don't want to wind up at the age of ninety saying, well, I may have watched a lot of TV. But I sure was safe."

Malfunction at 4,500 Feet

By: Eric Fair

No shit...there I was...thought I was going to die!

Me and Mike, the skydiving instructor who was buckled to my back, had just plummeted about 8,000 feet in less than a minute. The reassuring opening shock of our monster tandem canopy had just brought a smile to my lips. That's when I heard Mike say the one word I'd hoped I'd never hear while dangling underneath an inflated bag of nylon.

"Uh-oh!"

I couldn't believe my ears. My certified, qualified, and highly experienced tandem skydiving instructor had just said, "Uh-oh!"

I mean, there we were, drifting peacefully through space after nearly a minute of exhilarating, eye-watering 120-mile-per-hour free-fall and this guy strapped to my back is muttering "uh-oh" under his breath. I glanced at the altimeter on my wrist. We were a good 4,500 feet off the deck.

Being an experienced thrill-sport expert, I instinctively know that Mike's two-syllable assessment of our current situation had something to do with the lazy but definite right turn we seemed to be

stuck in. Calmly, with every intention of being as helpful as I could possibly be, I asked the only intelligent question I could think of.

"Yo, Mike!" I blurted. "You didn't just say 'uh-oh' did you?!"

Mike, who is Australian, picked that moment to call me "mate." I knew it was his way of saying that our fates had just become irrevocably intertwined. "We've got a bit of a problem, mate!" said Mike. "Our right side steering lines are tangled at the slider."

"Does that mean we can only turn right?" My inquiring mind wanted to know. "How are we gonna land if this thing is spiraling us to the right?"

"We can't," said Mike. "We have to see if we can fly straight without stalling. If we can we'll stick with this canopy. Otherwise, we'll have to cut away and go to our reserve."

"RESERVE?!" The very word sent shivers down my spine. Going to our reserve meant we'd first have to get rid of our main chute. Then we'd have to suffer through another mind-bending free-fall while we waited for the reserve—our last remaining parachute—to open and open properly. If it didn't, the stop at the end of our ride would be a sudden one—caused by the ground.

"We got some time," Mike said. "Let's try to fix this one."

"Yeah, let's!" I agreed. "What can I do?"

Mike told me to pull down on the left riser until we were flying straight. I did what he said while he tried to jerk the right side lines loose. In the meantime, I managed to keep us going straight all right—but at a speed that Mike said may or may not be good enough to bring us to earth under full control.

"We still got time," said Mike. "I'll keep trying." Mike's apparent unhappiness with our current canopy was beginning to concern me, especially since the altimeter on my wrist now said we were only 2,500 feet off the deck.

"Uh—Mike?" I queried. "You havin' any luck? We're getting kind of low!"

Mike offered some bad news and some good news. The risers were still most definitely tangled and were damned well going to stay that way. The good news was that we weren't going to have to play our last card—the reserve chute.

"We'll stick with this canopy," said Mike confidently—thank God. "We can make it fly straight and our descent isn't too bad. We should be all right. But you're going to have to help me flare (pull down hard on both sets of risers) on landing."

Believe me, I told Mike quite certainly that I just LOVED what he said and how he said it. The smile began to return to my lips and got bigger and bigger as we approached the ground. Mike's professional judgment had been right-on. We were flying straight and it honestly appeared as if our landing would be spectacularly uneventful.

Several feet off the deck, Mike yelled, "Pull hard! Now!" I heaved on the risers for all I was worth—touchdown. No jolts. No steps. I was so happy I burst out laughing.

"So, how'd ya like THAT?!" Mike's boss, obviously unaware of what had just transpired, yelled at me as he ran over to help us pack up. Good old Don was fully expecting to bathe in the excited babbling of yet another safely satisfied customer.

"We had a MALFUNCTION, Don!" I shot back, my eyes practically blazing with the afterglow and thrill of surviving what felt like a close call. "It was wonderful... Thanks for the freakin' ride!"

Don's mouth just dropped open.

It's a Man's World

By: Lynn Ferrin

A few pitches up the Royal Arches, we decided, would make a nice climb on this sultry summer afternoon in Yosemite Valley. We'd be down in time for a leisurely dinner and campfire and shmoozing around Camp Four under the August moon.

Ray was the ideal climbing partner for a novice like me; he hadn't fully recovered from his bone-smashing spill on the icewall at Nun Kun, and his leg was still in a brace. He still wasn't ready to go back to climbing with the big boys, but he liked keeping his skills honed, and anyway in those days he was one of the few honchos around Camp Four who was willing and nice enough to climb with females.

Now, the Royal Arches are very aesthetic, big curving granite overhangs, like the cloisters of medieval monasteries, on the northeast side of the valley, above the Ahwahnee Hotel. It's a nice walk over there, on the forest path that runs along the bottom of the valley walls.

Okay, so we rope up and Ray leads, placing pins—back then we were still using pitons. I'd follow and pull them out as I moved up the rock face. Also, instead of modern harnesses, we used just a wrapped-webbing "swami" belt about our waists for tying in. (A bit of background important to this story.)

125

Sanders, '93

I always enjoyed those times when it was my turn to belay Ray as he moved up, concentrating hard on the task at hand, but something in my mind always went off wool-gathering. I'd muse about how beautiful the place was, those waterfalls plunging down the silver walls into the wildflowers, and how climbers could be such bastards and how the good ones had no footsteps. I mean, you could never hear them approaching. But that's another story.

Anyway, we had done about three pitches, and I was tied in to a bolt and belaying Ray from a very minuscule ledge when I realized I shouldn't have guzzled so much lemonade before we started. When he got to the top of the pitch, I decided, I'd take care of it before I started climbing. He'd be out of sight above, and I couldn't see anyone below right then. But geeze, the ledge was only four inches wide at most, with solid rock behind it.

I know, I'd let him pull the rope tight and that would hold me in place while I sort of balanced with my toes on the ledge, facing the wall. Got that?

Okay, so he gets to the top of his pitch, yells that he's off belay, and ties himself in to start belaying me. "Ready to climb?" he calls a moment later. "Uh, not quite yet. But I'm on belay. Up rope!"

The rope pulls taut, I turn and face the wall. I yell for him to give me a little slack. So I can get into a comfortable squat, see.

"What are you doing?" he calls.

"Uh, nothing, I'll start in a second. But keep the rope tight."

Swami, buttons, zippers, layers of clothes. Gawd.

Success! Now then...

"Hey," comes his voice, "whaddaya doing."

I was almost finished. "Just a minute! I'll come up soon!"

For some reason he took that as a command to pull up the rope. It was just enough to knock me off balance.

I fell off the ledge, and swung at the end of my rope, on the wall high above the Ahwahnee Hotel, fragrante delicto, so to speak.

No shit, there I was.

Then I had to get back on the wall and inch my way up to the ledge from which I'd fallen. Did you ever try to rock-climb with your pants around your ankles?

Cassady Rock

By: Jim Cassady

No shit, there I was... at Staircase Rapid on the North Fork of the American in the spring of 1981, standing on a rock with my paddle in my hand. The raft I had been in seconds before was stuck in the hole at Middle Staircase with the crew being ejected like cowboys on rodeo bulls. On the shore were several boat loads of guides and passengers. I'm sure that they were concerned for our predicament at some level, but mostly they were rolling with laughter.

How did I get there? Was it a brilliant stroke of insight based on a split second response to a basic survival instinct or was it just a weenie abandoning ship. I'll answer the first question, you can make the call about the second.

I had the dream job that river runners yearn for, getting paid to explore rivers. The year before, I had taken my boss, Bill McGinnis, owner of the commercial raft company Whitewater Voyages, down the Forks of the Kern. He loved it and developed it as a commercial trip. When he was putting together his outfitting brochure for the next season, he asked me if I had made any more "discoveries." I subsequently added a few more adventures to the catalogue, including the North Fork of the American.

Over the winter, customers booked some trips onto the North Fork, so come spring we needed to train our guides on the river. While Bill was leading our first commercial trip on the North Fork, I was leading a guide's training trip at the same time.

We happened to meet at Staircase Rapid. The crews were experiencing a brutal day with raft after raft failing to execute the necessary move to the right, hitting the rock immediately before Middle Staircase, losing momentum, and then slowly sliding into the yawning hole to get annihilated. It was ugly!

My crew, a raft full of guides, was instructed to perform an upstream ferry while backpaddling which would allow us to make the necessary move to the right between Upper and Middle Staircase. It looked to be a piece of cake. Not! Our "official" guide for the rapid, Bob Day, was guiding from the rear right while I sat next to him at rear left. We went through Upper Staircase without incident and began backpaddling. Unfortunately, we didn't have the necessary angle to ferry successfully to the right. We bumped slowly into the rock to the left side of the river, just above the hole at the middle drop—this was not good! Realizing our fate was sealed, now seemed to be as good a time as any to step out onto the available rock—the one we had just bumped into. It was a split second decision and my body reacted. My crew went down while I observed—as any instructor should.

Brilliant or cowardly, you make the call. Be it known that the rock was officially named after me, Cassady Rock. Bob Day gave me a commemorative plaque, including pictures of that fateful day—it still hangs on my wall.

Cataract Canyon

By: Jeff Bennett

Get in a raft with a river guide and you're likely to hear enough tall tales to fill a novel. Some of them are true. For me, it always helps to keep a healthy supply of enduring stories in my repartee to fill in quiet moments, flat stretches, and to avoid questions like, "how deep's this river?"

While the best river stories usually stem from first hand experiences, a good secondhand tale can't be overlooked. Such is the case with the following story.

During my early days as a raft guide, I had the good fortune of befriending an ex-Colorado River guide. All his boating skills were acquired while getting his raft stomped by the big rapids of Cataract Canyon, which, during high water, is one of the most treacherous sections of the Colorado. Though the end result was a fine set of well-honed big water skills, his initiation to the business of running rivers was downright embarrassing.

The swamper is the low man on the guiding totem pole. Swampers load and unload rafts, set up porta-potties, and fill the position of an all around "gofer." In Cataract Canyon, swampers hang out by the guides, watching their every move, sometimes waiting years for the moment when they can take the helm.

Arnie had just bluffed his way into his first river job, swamping for a big outfitter of marginal repute. His verbal resume had

131

consisted of trips from the Rogue down to the Stanislaus, with a few rivers in between.

Arnie spent the beginning of his first season swamping during high water trips through Cataract. During the peak of runoff, raft companies sent motorized pontoon boats or triple-rigs through the big drops. This allowed for a greater margin of safety, but imparted nothing upon the swamper. After a couple of these trips, Arnie split for the Colorado Rockies for a few weeks of backpacking.

Upon his return, he was surprised to find things had changed. A guide strike was on and the company was understaffed. The top two-thirds of the totem pole had been hacked off. Arnie was now a head boatsman.

A trip was heading out the next day, and Arnie's services were badly needed. "You want to guide it?" asked the owner. "The river's still high. It's a real scream in there. But these folks really want an oar trip, you up to it?"

Arnie hadn't expected that question quite so fast. His expertise was dishwater, not whitewater. But Arnie was quick on his toes. This was an opportunity that had to be grabbed. "Uhm, well, uhm..." If he was going to do this trip, he'd have to say yes before his throat totally sealed off. "...e rr, yeah."

Arnie was now locked in. No turning back. He dragged his knotted stomach over to a friend's house and bummed some beer.

"Hey, Arnie, I heard you're going to row tomorrow."

"Yep."

"One trip just got back. A real nightmare. They lined up wrong at Satan's Gut and flipped, big time. Everyone held onto the raft. And with the oars and ammo cans and all, some folks got pretty banged up. A couple of broken arms or legs or something. Yeah, a real nightmare."

Arnie's mind was spinning. Flips...oars...broken arms. He was starting to wish he had been on the level about his expertise. Or lack thereof. But, it was too late. By the time the morning arrived, he found himself on a bus heading toward the put-in.

The first couple of days of most Cataract Canyon trips take in miles of peaceful water, easy rapids, and glorious scenery. While the passengers partook in these casual observations, Arnie honed his rowing skills. He pulled on the left oar, then on the right. Anyone who knew anything would have wondered what the heck Arnie was doing working up a sweat in Class II water. But, he was pulling it off. He told stories from his first Cataract trips as if he'd done it for years. Everyone was convinced of Arnie's skills—except Arnie.

After a couple of days on the river, they had reached the lip of the inevitable. The granddaddies of Cataract Canyon rapids—Mile Long and The Big Drop. Arnie's heart was wrestling his stomach for a position in his throat. A creeping fear began to take over the thought centers in his brain. "What the hell am I doing here?" he thought. Meanwhile, his mouth moved with the disguise of confidence which he had perfected over the course of the last two days of guiding.

Flying through Mile Long, Arnie's oars danced along the surface like wounded crickets, catching the current and the tips of waves, and flailing in the troughs. But, he was doing all right. Hanging tough and keeping the raft straight.

Before long, it was all over. Arnie and his crew had survived Mile Long, slurping down their victory like so many shots of confidence. But more rapids—worse rapids—waited downstream.

Arnie's biggest moment came way too soon. Quivering with excitement and terror, he went into a short guide's speech he'd heard the old timers say before: "Okay, down there is Satan's Seat and Satan's Gut. The Big Drop. It's what we are here for. Remember everything about what I said when we started this trip. Don't panic, hold on tight, and DON'T FALL OUT. "

Following final preparations, Arnie tugged heavily on the oars, straining hard to get the boat out into the main current. Soon, truck-sized walls of water began dancing like angry spirits on the river's surface. Arnie's mind was becoming overloaded. "A real nightmare...lining up wrong...flipped...held onto the raft...broken arms...broken arms...broken arms." His friend's words rang loudly above the roar of the rapids. Then, it happened.

"SNAP!" An oar let go with a sickening pop. "KAPLOOSH!" The first set of waves exploded over the boat, nearly capsizing the raft. Paralyzed with fear, Arnie could do nothing. Huge diagonal waves reached skyward, forming narrow corridors of doom, funneling the raft and crew towards extinction.

"JUMP!"

The crew looked startled.

"C'MON! JUMP!!"

Arnie had gone berserk. No one could have guessed what was running through his mind. The perceived inevitability of a flip in Satan's Gut had warped Arnie's sense of judgment. He felt that it would be better to simply swim the Gut than to hold onto a tumbling raft full of arm-breaking oars and ammo cans.

"J-U-U-U-M-P!"

No one budged an inch. For many of the passengers, this was their first taste of wilderness adventure. This was supposed to be fun. Exciting. Not a Hollywood version of "Arnie Goes Psycho." They hunkered lower and lower into the raft, holding onto ropes and frames with white-knuckled vengeance.

"JUMP!"

Arnie went overboard. No kidding! Right there in the middle of Mother Nature's personal drowning pool. Out there under the vultures and Utah's blazing sun.

It took a few seconds before Arnie found surface again. He came up within earshot of the raft. Seeing his crew glued in place, he shouted his final words of misguided encouragement before concerns for his own well being became paramount.

"JUMP!" Blub, blub, blub, blub, blub...

Now the raft, totally unguided, floated perilously toward Cataract Canyon's biggest, ugliest holes. Nearby, Arnie bobbed through the churning brown waters like a cork in a sea storm. Both raft and Arnie had the worst of possible lines. A big hole drew near. The roar of the water was sickening.

In a moment it was all over. Somehow, the raft had slipped through unscathed. The crew was safe. A perfect run. But, Arnie was nowhere to be found.

"There he is!" shouted someone from the raft.

Arnie had taken an awful swim. He had entered the hole straight on, dead center. He was no match for its powerful grasp. He was sent deep into the bowels of the Colorado once, tumbled and released, and sucked back down for another ride. By the time he had reached the calm pools below, he had expended all the energy he had in his fight for survival.

"Arnie, hang in there. Just a second." One of the least adventurous passengers—a true city-slicker—had unstrapped a spare oar and set out on rescuing Arnie.

By that time, other boats had converged for the rescue, but Arnie's crew reached him first. They hauled him over the gunwales and laid him on the pile of gear, letting the sun revive him.

By the time he came around, there was little left to Arnie's Cataract Canyon trip. The peaceful calm of Lake Powell waited downstream. There would be no opportunity for vindication. No chance to replenish his ego. Just hour after hour of the longest days of Arnie's life.

His story reached near legendary proportions in some circles. Quite an unwelcome infamy. Fortunately, his real name is seldom revealed...

Attack Beaver at 6,000 Feet

By: Dennis Bitton

Johnny and Mike drove the truck down the rutted road through the sagebrush. Everything in the truck got bounced around a bit. When they finally pulled across the bridge to the ranch house on Johnny's uncle's land, it was two o'clock.

"Right on schedule," noted Mike.

"Yeah," said Johnny, "we'll just swing left to the east here and go down through the pasture for about a half mile. The river splits just above here so we'll be fishing just part of the total flow, and it should give us a good chance at some fair-sized fish with easy wading."

"How's your heart?" asked Mike.

"It's OK," Johnny said with a little irritation. He didn't like being reminded about his health problems in the middle of a day's fishing.

"Doesn't this high altitude get to you?" wondered Mike. "How high up are we anyway?"

Sanders, '93

"We're over 6,000 feet right here," replied Johnny. "This morning, up in the high country, that whole valley floor was right around 8,000 feet."

"No wonder I felt a little winded," said Mike. "And it doesn't poop you out?"

"Nah, the doctor said that a weak heart just doesn't circulate the blood very well. The difference in oxygen at altitude doesn't matter as much as what my heart's doing on its own. Actually, just being outside in the fresh air makes me feel better than being indoors, even at high elevation."

"You sure you don't want to take a rest?" asked Mike. "I could use one. In fact, if you don't mind, I think I'd like to take a little siesta."

"That's fine, I've got a foam pad in the back of the truck. You can lie there or take the pad over to the willows and lie down in the shade there."

"OK, I'll do that . . . you still going fishing?"

"Yep. I'll wander downstream a bit and see what's cooking. You come on down behind me. If I get tired, I'll come back upstream. That way, we won't miss each other. Still want to get out of here about dark?"

"Suits me. You say it's about two hours back to town?"

"Yeah, but we can stop at a little place about halfway there and get some supper. Great food, in a rough sort of way."

"OK, I'll take a nap. You go fishing and I'll come and get you later."

"All right, see you in a bit."

Johnny headed off down the stream. Locals call it a river, even the maps call it a river—Lost River to be exact—because it wandered out into the desert and disappeared as it sank into the ground. Johnny had been coming here since he was a little kid, with his Dad.

He knew where he was going. There was an irrigation ditch his uncle had cut out with a Cat just below here. Below that was a series of deep cut banks. Half a dozen or more in just a half mile.

He'd drift a nymph through the deep water on the bends. If nothing happened there, it wasn't going to happen anywhere today.

Johnny crossed the irrigation ditch and watched the upstream sedimentation ("we used to call it mud," thought Johnny with a smile) swirling around his neoprene waders. It collected there because his uncle's diversion dam backed up the stream's fines ("another great word!" thought Johnny) and they settled there.

Below the dam the main flow of the current switched from the left hand bank to the right bank, moving on downstream. That meant the water was flowing almost due east here, and as Johnny looked that way, he again felt the mind lifting experience of gazing at those mountains. The Lost River Range.

Johnny didn't tell too many people, but he thought about those mountains a lot. During the work week, when things were frantic, he'd picture the mountains and know they'd be there if he needed to come back. When he'd been in the hospital he'd thought about them, and just as soon as he'd gotten out, he had come here, and they'd helped.

"I'm glad you're there and I'm glad Mike's having a good time," Johnny thought to the mountains, " but I'd really appreciate it if you could get us into a few more fish." Johnny knew it was a little weird talking to mountains, but he did it all the time. He'd talk to mountains, trees, fence posts and even deer, antelopes and jackrabbits if he saw them. He'd been doing it since he was a kid, and it was one childish thing he didn't want to let go of. So he kept talking.

"What fly do I try now?" he asked the surrounding cottonwoods. Hearing no answer, he reached for the fly on his cork rod grip. It was the Prince Nymph. It had done a fair job for him this morning, but he'd broken off the tippet several times, and he only had about six inches of it left.

"I'd better change that," he said to himself, now that he was talking about something significant. "If I don't, sure as Hades some big fish will hit it and break me off."

He broke off the fly. Reached into his vest for a new tapered leader and took the old one off, clear up at his butt material, just off the fly line. Nine feet of new leader, tapered down to a four pound test, would be just about right.

As Johnny was tying a loop in his new leader, he noticed a small animal swimming upstream just across the stream. It was dark colored and so low in the water he couldn't tell exactly what it was, but judging from the size and the rate it was swimming, he'd guess muskrat.

Johnny finished tying the loop, connected that to the loop of his butt material and tied on a new Prince Nymph. Maybe the fish would appreciate its fresh appearance. As he turned to go downstream, he noticed a beaver swimming upstream towards him on his side of the stream. "Strange," thought Johnny, "It's awfully shallow there. How can he swim there?"

Just then the beaver pulled itself up on its feet and started walking upstream. It was enormous. Johnny couldn't remember ever seeing one any bigger. It was the size of a German shepherd, probably weighed over 40 pounds. And, it was headed straight for Johnny.

"What's going on?" he thought. "Where's he going?"

Fascinated, Johnny just stood there and watched. The beaver kept plodding upstream. It couldn't have been easy in that current. The big beaver sort of lumbered along. "If he weren't so big, you might call it waddling," he smiled.

The beaver was getting close now, no more than 20 feet away. "I'd better scare him off," thought Johnny.

Johnny found a small piece of driftwood, and lobbed it just in front of the beaver. He pitched it underhand with a little arch to it so that it went up and came down right in front of the beaver's nose. The beaver snorted, shook his head and moved back into the faster current.

"That's that," thought Johnny. "I wonder what he thought he was going to do?"

Holding the Prince Nymph in his left hand, and his rod in his right, he started downstream. The beaver was swimming downstream now too, against the far bank. Johnny felt better.

But, as Johnny stepped into the water, the beaver turned left, headed crosscurrent and was back on Johnny's side of the stream. Then it turned upstream, and headed straight for him again.

"This is crazy," thought Johnny. "He's coming at me again." And he was definitely coming at him. Straight upstream, right on line. No doubt.

Johnny could feel his heart start to beat faster. He'd had heart problems for three years now, Cardiomyopathy, they called it. He wasn't supposed to lift anything very heavy and was to avoid strenuous exercise. He had learned how to fish "easy," so he had that covered, but this beaver was another matter.

It was still coming at him, now just 20 feet away again. Johnny turned around to move on upstream and ran right into the wild rose bush thicket he'd forgotten about. That blocked his way upstream and up the bank. All he had left was out into the stream or down the near bank, side stepping the beaver—assuming it didn't lunge.

Johnny ran. He ran on his tippy toes around the beaver, which was no match for his adrenaline-fed fear, and was into the water below and behind the beaver in seconds. On the way by, he took a quick look at the beaver's mouth to see if there was any foam there. Maybe this critter was rabid.

"Wouldn't that be a pip!" thought Johnny out loud.

But there was no sign of foam and no evidence of a tortured mind, just a determined one. The beaver was definitely chasing Johnny.

He waded downstream 80 feet or so, crossed the 20 foot stream and climbed up a 10 foot bank. He turned to check on the beaver, and it was following. Johnny retreated 40 feet back into the willows and cottonwoods to make sure he was well off the stream bank, just in case that was all the beaver was interested in.

Standing there, gasping for breath, he felt foolish and scared at the same time.

"What are you doing, running away from a beaver?" he asked himself. "It's silly, and your heart doesn't need the excitement or the exercise."

"Tell me about it," he said, now genuinely talking to himself in earnest. "I could die here, running away from a mad beaver. This is so stupid. Get a grip, what are you going to do?"

"Well," he said to himself, "if he comes up the bank, you know he's definitely after you and not just acting strange on the stream. If he shows, you had better club him."

Looking around, he found no clubs, so he gathered six or seven good-sized rocks, about the size of softballs, each weighing over a pound.

"That'll stop him," he said to himself, finally starting to catch his breath and calm down a little. Just then the beaver crested the edge of the bank, and started waddling right towards him. Johnny let fly with a rock. It was wide by three feet.

"Heck of a note," he told himself. "You're going to get bit because you can't throw a softball. I'll wait until he gets closer."

At 15 feet, he let fly again, and missed again. "That's pathetic!" he told himself. "Now what?"

At ten feet, the beaver presented an easy target. Johnny threw low and hard and cracked the beaver right over its eye. He saw one paw go up, and he felt bad. When the beaver went down and started thrashing around, Johnny felt worse. But, the beaver managed to get up, apparently none the worse for the wear and suddenly honestly disinterested in Johnny, it hightailed it to the river and swam downstream quickly.

Johnny, thinking to himself that this was crazy, decided to head back to the truck and rest. Back upstream, by the irrigation ditch, he ran into Mike coming downstream.

"How's the fishing?"

"You won't believe what just happened to me," replied Johnny. "I was attacked by a beaver. It chased me downstream and up the bank and I had to hit it in the head with a rock to get it to back off."

"No kidding? He still down there?"

"Yeah. I'm heading back to the truck to rest."

"I'll come with you," said Mike. "I sure don't want to go wandering down through the trees if he's still down there. By the way, how's your heart?"

"Better," replied Johnny. "Fishing always makes it better."

Deliverance Remembered

By: Jim Cassady

I was fourteen years old in an aluminum rental canoe going hell-bent down the rapids of the Potomac River that summer of 1960. If there ever was a classic formula that spelled trouble, this was it—a bunch of teenagers with the summer off, craving adventure, and lacking the knowledge or maturity to find it without getting into trouble.

It all started innocently enough. On a blisteringly hot day, we took the bus down to Fletcher's Boathouse and rented a canoe. We paddled on the C&O Canal until we got to a lock and a sign saying "No Rental Canoes Beyond This Point." Off to the west, beyond the sign were beautiful woodlands past which one could hear the distant rumble of the Potomac River. Heck, it was summertime and we were teenagers with too much time on our hands and a big thirst for adventure. What else could we do?

That's right, we carried the canoe through the woods to the Potomac. We started out feeling good, floating along on moving water. The moving water became swiftly moving water, then ripples, then rapids. We were in heaven. The excitement! The exhilaration! It was wonderful. Capsize? Who cared—we were young and

Sanders, '93

immortal. At the end of the rapids we carried the canoe up and ran them again.

I can't remember exactly how many times we shot the Potomac rapids that summer. The last time I do recall losing my glasses and a friend of mine received a large bruise on his thigh. That kind of put a stop to our canoeing adventures for the season. The next summer, my family moved to California and I forgot about the thrill of whitewater, until the movie *Deliverance* that is, which drew me back in—this time for good.

Thirteen years later found me on the Merced River on a Memorial Day weekend, 1973, in an open canoe without float bags—the river flow was about 10,000 cfs. I had absolutely no business being there. I was 27 and had a "master of the universe" attitude. In reality, I didn't have a clue. How did I get in such a bad predicament?

It was Hollywood's fault. My best friend, Erik Fair, and I saw the movie, *Deliverance*. Erik was my age with a similar bent for excitement. In the movie's terms, we were definitely Jon Voight types, but constantly yearned to be Burt Reynolds. We naturally went and purchased an aluminum canoe and I spent my days dreaming of whitewater.

There were no good guidebooks at that time to California rivers so I went down to the library to scan the topo maps. Using this exhaustive research, we went out and ran the Kern, Tule, and Kings. Big fun for me. Erik, however, questioned my judgment about little things like ferrying across the river at the lip of a 20-foot waterfall. He drifted out of boating into something he felt more comfortable with—hang gliding.

Me, I was stoked on whitewater and thought I was an expert because I'd seen the movie three times. I had heard that the Merced was a good river so I convinced my brother-in-law to come with me. Memorial Day weekend looked good. In my thinking, the river would be low because it was hot and it hadn't rained in a while. I had not been introduced to the concept of snowmelt and runoff just yet.

We got to the river and man, did it seem like a lot of water. Still, we had come all the way from Southern California and not putting in the river just because there was a question of safety was never considered. My brother-in-law and I thought we were well prepared with our horse-collar lifejackets, sneakers, and suntan lotion. We put in confidently. We stayed upright for, oh, say about two hundred yards. My brother-in-law made an intelligent and quick exit to the shore.

Me, I watched him swim to safety as I barreled around the first bend clinging to the canoe. I figured I would just shove it into the first available eddy—at 10,000 cfs with no float bags. Right! The following 10 minutes seemed like an hour. A car horn from some guys who had apparently been following me along the highway drew my attention. Leaving the canoe began to seem like a good idea, so I pushed off, clung to a rock for awhile and then struggled out of the river. Dripping everywhere, I dove into the car which set off in hot pursuit of the now unmanned canoe.

At the Briceburg Bridge we were ahead of the canoe. Thinking quickly, though still not altogether clearly, I tied a rope to the bridge and readied myself to leap into the river after the canoe. Fortunately, it whisked by without so much as a wave. Otherwise, the headlines might have read, "Man dies tied to bridge while attempting to save canoe."

There was nothing left to do but pick up my car and brother-in-law and wait for my canoe to show up downstream at the top of the reservoir. It never showed—maybe it was being held captive by Hillbillies. I headed home, with my tail tucked between my legs.

Yak Attack at 16,000 Feet

By: Ken Hanley

I'd been carrying the message for about a month and a half. The letter was bent, a bit frayed around the edges, even some of the ink had begun to fade. I was just a few hours away from being face to face with the Honorable Rinpoche Lakpa.

Rinpoche usually resided in a tiny monastery located in the farthest reaches of the Langtang region. His temple was tucked away in the folds of the massive mountains surrounding the upper Langtang Khola, a beautiful river born in the iceflows of Tibet. I was told that if he wasn't in the monastery, he would surely be found at his hermitage. It was a small cave somewhere near the base of Kyungka Ri.

It all sounded simple enough, just put one foot in front of the other and head northeast into the high country. There was one rub however. This time, in Langtang, Kyungka Ri and the upper valley were off limits to trekkers. The Nepali-Tibetan border was considered a politically sensitive area, and the Rinpoche's cave fell smack dab within the restricted zone!

The Red Guard was making life miserable for anyone venturing close to their outposts. Here I was, halfway around the planet, fac-

ing a stalemate enforced by China's watchdogs . . . this was unacceptable! I had to deliver the letter.

Staying at Dorje's hut, I mused over the situation. Why was I chosen to deliver such a message of import? Why would I be allowed to travel so far and not complete the task? Was it a spiritual test, part of the quest? I couldn't seem to find an answer for any of the questions I posed. Maybe I was meant to just sit here, surrounded by the shrouded summits, listening to silent music.

A few days passed and Dorje introduced me to Mingmar Sherpa. Mingmar was a yak herder turned interpreter, just the kinda guy I needed to gain access to the restricted zone. He had heard I needed to see the Lama Rinpoche. He was willing to help me in any way. Outstanding!

Mingmar assured me that with all his family contacts I'd have no problem reaching the cave. He just asked me to keep an open mind, and be prepared to travel during the night. No problem.

During my journey into the high country (this season), I'd been experiencing some elimination problems. It was common for trekkers to come down with "The Trots," "The Quick Step," "The Squirts." My dilemma was quite the opposite. I had a fully developed case of "The Clamp!" Constipation in the Himalayas was about as rare as a day at the beach, and between the Red Guard and The Clamp, I was beginning to wear my frustration on my sleeves.

It had been hard for me to get a solid night's sleep for some time now. Tossing and turning seemed to consume most of my restless nights. Finally, drifting off somewhere between unwanted reality and welcome dreamscapes, I felt a hand tapping at my leg. It was Mingmar. It was time to leave. Figures as much—it had just been one of those weeks.

Pulling myself together, I followed Mingmar into the pasture. The celestial show was magnificent. What a privilege it was to be standing here, it was truly an amazing site to behold. The wind was just a whisper. Moonglow bathed the valley. I could see the mountain's silhouette, a gentle reminder that we still had a task to complete.

Walking in the moon's brilliance had been a piece of cake. Hours had passed. I'm not sure how many. I could make out a small structure in the distance. We had come upon another yak herder's hut. It was nothing more than a simple frame of branches, bent over to form a tunnel, and covered with a few thick hides. Mingmar and I crawled inside. I really felt at peace in the humble refuge. Closing my eyes, there was no problem drifting into fantasies of the world beyond wakeful borders.

Sunbeams filtered through some minor holes in the yak hide; just enough to announce the new day's arrival. Leaning out the hut I could see a herd of yak grazing on the sparsely grown alpine grasses. It was time to get up and take care of business. I'd lost count of how many days it'd been without a "BM." Definitely time to try again. I grabbed my daypack and headed off to find a suitable throne room.

Winding my way through the yak pasture I found a likely spot to set up shop. There were stones of various sizes laying about, a few looked large enough to actually build a pretty decent throne. I began stacking them in a small ringed fashion and before long had completed a place to park my buns.

Any mountaineer can tell you trying to have a simple "movement" at altitude just ain't easy. The higher you go, the more your body says no. This was no picnic.

I glanced down at my watch, it had been about fifteen minutes. I noticed there was a particular yak that was uneasy with me in the pasture. Just what I needed, a yak with an attitude. I couldn't believe this was happening to me. Attempting to refocus myself to the task at hand, I kept bearing down trying to get some results. No such luck. In fact, I was beginning to feel lightheaded. My blood pressure was dropping. My legs were even beginning to fall asleep. Damn!

The yak had moved closer to me and started to become more aggressive. Great! Now what? Charge the yak with my pants at half mast? I could still reach some of the stones laying at my feet. I bent down to collect a few and felt like passing out. Whoa! Here I am; stuck on a stone throne with "The Clamp," on the verge of passing out, and being harassed by a squirrelly yak. To make matters worse, after I throw these few stones at the irritable cuss, I won't be able to reach any more ammo. What a drag?

It had become a battle of will. The yak kept threatening to charge. I kept firing away. Without any better alternative, I was

reduced to the stones I was sitting on!! One by one I was disman-
tling the very throne I needed for relief. Is there no justice in the
world? My bowels were as tight as a guitar string. With a ton of
angry beast in my face it was impossible to calm down.

Time was just ticking away. I'd glance at my watch. Look up at
the yak. Fire off a stone, and sigh in disgust. The yak became more
obnoxious. Now I was sinking into the toilet. The sun beat down on
me. I was yelling for help. Where the hell was Mingmar, couldn't
he see I've got my butt in a sling?

I began to imagine some preposterous headlines: "Mountaineer
Gets Stomped In The Throne Room Of The Gods!" "Godzilla
Meets Bambi At 16,000 Feet." What if they print my name in the
story. Oh God. Everyone will know I was mashed into a Yak-
patty...this really sucks.

Over forty minutes had lapsed. I could feel the energy just slip
out of my body. No more power to poop. No more will to fight. Just
when I thought I was going to give in to the thought of getting
trampled by a tank, I heard a sharp crack come from behind me. At
the same moment a stone drilled into the yak's flank. He gave way
with a snort and a jump. I looked over my shoulder. Mingmar was
loading another stone into the small pocket of his yak herder's
sling. Like David against Goliath, this little guy was whipping that
sling around and getting real results!

As the yak trotted off to shake the sting from Mingmar's skillful
hand, I tried to regain my composure. The shear indignity of it all
was beginning to get real old. Lord, just let me drop a load. Mingmar had brought a cup of instant coffee into the field. I remember
coffee being a diuretic. Slurping down the warmed brew I prayed
this would be the ticket that turns things around. Just a few seconds
had passed and I could feel my lower half relax...no more
spasms...no more obstructions...just warm relief...ah sweet victory! I could finally get on with my life.

Returning to the hut we gathered our belongings and set off for
our meeting with the Lama. I didn't realize we were only moments
away from Rinpoche's sanctuary. As we approached the cave we
were greeted with strings of colorful prayer flags. The breeze carrying their message over the land and high into the heavens.

Mingmar entered first. I waited outside. A moment passed and he returned smiling, extending his hand. At that very moment I knew I was in the presence of a higher being. The journey was worth it (in all of its toil and grace), I was about to be sitting with a man of vision and extraordinary inner peace. With the letter in my hand, I took a deep breath and entered a world beyond . . .

Buried in an Island of Safety

By: Peter Whittaker with Andrea Gabbard

No shit, there I was, up to my neck in snow and stuck in a tree.

I was able to lift my head enough to watch the avalanche rumble on down the slope another seven or eight hundred feet and hit the group of clients who were in what they thought was an "island of safety." Oddly enough, the first thing I hear is Chuck, our helicopter pilot, coming through on my radio, which has miraculously remained attached to me.

"I can see him, I can see him," Chuck is shouting. "He's stuck behind a tree."

Stuck is right. Not more than a couple of minutes ago, I had agreed to check out a slope for avalanche danger. As the tailgunner, or rear guide, of a helicopter ski outfit, I had waited up top while Darwin, the head guide, took our party of eight skiers down a steep powder slope. We knew there was a hazard out there, what heli ski guides would call a "moderate hazard," but we were managing it. Or so it appeared. Darwin and the rest of the party had skied down without mishap.

Darwin had radioed back up to me: "Hey, Pete, take a look at that other aspect, as an option for the next run."

155

Sanders, '93

So many things can change when you're on a mountain of snow. You might have a really solid layer of white powder, but the sun and the orientation of the slope can make the difference between one that is secure and one that's about to break off.

That's exactly what happened. I skied over to check out this slope, turned my skis downhill, got two turns into it and suddenly this thing pulled out and totally surprised me. It pulled out about a hundred feet behind me as I was skiing. My first indication that something was wrong was when the whole slope began sliding, moving to the left. As I'm turning, all of a sudden I find myself on my right hip, but I haven't fallen!

I'm thinking, "This is weird," and then I look around and realize, Holy Shit, I'm in an avalanche.

I knew I was in deep shit and I was going down fast. I'm on my hip and the thing starts to break up. First, it's one big piece, but as it picks up speed it's starting to fracture and froth. I'm sinking down deeper into it. Accumulating speed.

I try to get up with my head, to look, because I can feel that I'm picking up speed. All this is happening in the first few seconds. I'm getting up on my hands and having trouble breathing, from all the powder froth. I'm not that deep in the avalanche but there's so much frothing and out-of-control washing machine action going on that it's all I can do to just keep my head above it to watch where I'm going. I know there are trees ahead.

I lose it. I'm in it, out of control. I get swept another couple hundred feet, then slammed into a stand of trees. I'm wrapped around one, my head going downhill on one side, my legs on the other, with the full force of the avalanche pressing against me. I feel tremendous pressure, as though my life is being squeezed out of me, but it lets up just before I feel I might black out.

Now, I'm stuck in a tree with the ski party in danger below me. I've had major wind knocked out of me and can hardly talk. Darwin has located most of the party. The next thing I hear on the radio is that one of the skiers, a seventeen-year-old girl, is missing, buried somewhere. I think, "Shit, Whittaker, good job, you kicked off this avalanche and not only messed yourself up, but now there's a girl buried in it."

I finally caught my breath and was able to reach my radio. The first thing I said, being at the time the macho-guide-stud-bolt, was, "Bring my skis back up to me. I'll ski out of here." My skis, gloves and poles had been ripped off by the force of the avalanche. My gloves were found later, down below, completely inside out.

The year before, I had just come back from the 1984 Everest expedition led by my father, Lou Whittaker. I had been able to spend a bunch of nights above 25,000 feet. I was twenty-five years old, strong and healthy. I'd just quit ski patrol at Snowbird and Greg Smith, the helicopter ski service owner, heard about it and offered me a job as a heli ski guide. I said, "Sure." I knew it was a really great job. And, a perfect off-season job for me. During summers, I worked as a guide on Mt. Rainier in Washington, with my father's guide service, Rainier Mountaineering, Inc.

So, I'm back from the Himalayas and feeling pretty cocky. Feeling like I've been around, been on the big mountains and all. I had been working as a rookie heli ski guide for a month when the avalanche happened.

Your first year, you learn an awful lot. You listen a lot. I'd had a lot of experience skiing because I'd grown up skiing and climbing. But heli guiding was a new thing and I spent most of my time at the rear of the ski party, where, in the hierarchy of heli skiing, rookies belong.

I knew a lot about avalanches, having grown up with Mt. Rainier as my backyard playground. I had even survived an avalanche that my dad had kicked off accidentally while we were climbing together, and, a few years later, watched in horror as a major ice fall buried eleven climbers. You learn quickly to pay attention to what a mountain is trying to tell you.

Even so, even with an understanding of the risk involved and the objective hazards present, things can get out of control in an instant. Before you can even think to react.

In helicopter ski guiding, we do what they call "slope evaluation." In addition to the many tests used to determine what the potential for avalanche is, we also conduct tests by throwing bombs out of the helicopter onto the slopes.

The year I started at Snowbird, we had a great heli pilot named Chuck. He had been shot down twice in 'Nam and had more mountain hours than any other pilot in the U.S. An unbelievable pilot.

We carried thirty bombs in the back of this Bell Jet Ranger. You sit with a case of bombs between your legs, all set with 90-second fuses. The first time I was bombardier, the head guide sat up front with the pilot and another guide sat to my right to hand me bombs. Each bomb is a two-pound hand charge. A mix used at most ski areas. Packs a pretty good punch.

The head guide figures out beforehand where we're going to fly to test slopes. Not only the slopes we'll be skiing on, but also the ones above us. The Wasatch Mountains are 11,000 feet or so, and Chuck flies us in and out and around the peaks, so we can get a look at different couloirs and slopes that we might want to ski.

I swear to God, Chuck's reaction to the first pull of the spitter on the bomb—the initial smell of sulfur in the cockpit—was predatory. He starts flying like we're in 'Nam, diving and buzzing the slopes.

We pick a slope to test. Chuck gets the helicopter in position. Darwin yells, "Ready?" I yell back, "Ready!" He yells, "Go!" I pull the spitter on the bomb and suddenly realize that I'm holding a live bomb in my hands. It's a strange feeling.

There's a little window in the helicopter. I stick my arm out of it and wait for Darwin's commands. You don't throw the bombs, just drop them. Darwin is real good. When he yells "Now!" I drop a bomb. We do several in quick succession. Your adrenaline starts pumping. You've got to synchronize, not pull the spitter and drop the bomb on the floor of the cockpit in your hurry to get it out the window.

This is the safe way to check for avalanche danger. After we drop the charges, we hover over the area and listen to the bombs go off—sounds like "poof!" from the distance. Poof! A big crater appears in the side of the mountain. Poof! Black powder marks. Poof!—and the head guide yells, "It's going!" We've got an avalanche.

It's a classic slab avalanche. When it releases, you know that the underlayer has failed and you've got hundreds of yards of snow, a huge area, collapsing at the same time. It actually begins pulling away and moving as one piece. There's a fracture on top and one on the bottom. The whole piece kicks out and starts moving.

Some of these releases are between eight and twelve feet deep. That's a big avalanche. You watch these things start to come down first as one piece, then, as they pick up speed, they begin to break apart. The front turns into a wave.

Chuck likes to turn the ship around and fly right above the powder cloud. This avalanche we kicked off is going a hundred-forty miles an hour and that's just about as fast as the helicopter will go.

You realize that it's not the snow that's knocking over trees, it's the air blast that precedes the wave. Just shatters some of the trees. We ride above the avalanche, screaming down through a canyon.

Sometimes, a smaller avalanche will check itself when it first starts, and, if you're in it, you have time to point your skis downhill and actually get going faster than the slide. Get your speed up and try to do a big sweep turn and get out of the way. I've been able to do that a few times, ski out of the way. Sometimes, it works, and the danger passes you by. You feel like you're on a magic carpet ride. It's a tough call, though.

Another time, I was up near the starting zone and the fracture was only two or three feet uphill from my skis and I felt it start to go. I didn't have any room to sweep to the side, so I hammered my skis into the snow, trying to break down the slab beneath me. It worked. Everything else below me broke off and went sliding and I was left, just standing there. That technique came to me at that instant, out of a sense of self-preservation, I think. You know, when seconds count...

I've heard people give advice about what to do if you see an avalanche heading towards you. Like, "The first thing you do is take your skis off, then take off your poles..." and I picture some guy taking time to do this and waiting for the avalanche to hit him. On skis, you're pretty mobile. If you have a few seconds, you can usually move into a good position, such as behind a tree or just get out of the way.

If you get hit, though, staying on the surface is what you want to try to do. If it's a big avalanche and it really gets going, you're at the mercy of the slide. You're going to feel like you're in a washing machine, out of control. You just hope you don't hit anything.

The idea is to have your hands up around your face when you finally stop, to create a little air pocket. Maybe you can dig, too. Get out of your skis and poles, if they haven't been torn off you. Often, you'll be near enough the surface and can pop out.

When I got wrapped around that tree, I was lucky that my head was above the snow. A lot of people aren't so lucky and they suffocate.

I didn't realize until later how broken up I was. After about ten minutes, while I was waiting to be rescued, I realized that I was bleeding internally. I could feel swelling in the left side of my abdomen. I was beginning to feel incredible pain, but I told the guides that I could maintain while they rescued the girl.

They found her in just a few minutes, thanks to the avalanche beepers we all were wearing, which emit a signal you can pick up through the snow on a receiver. She had been caught but not carried at the toe of the avalanche. She was down almost three feet. Face down, her skis had been ripped off and her legs were bent all the way up, almost touching the back of her head. At first, they thought she was really messed up. She wasn't breathing. But, they ventilated her, got her breathing.

Nice thing about this situation is, you've got the ambulance right there—the helicopter noses in and they carefully load the girl in the ship and Chuck flies her to the hospital in Salt Lake City in about six minutes.

In the meantime, the guides begin their rescue effort on me. By the time they get me dug out, the helicopter is back and takes me in. I spend a few days in intensive care, waiting to find out if my spleen will be removed. It's ruptured. My ribs are broken, my knee is blown out, but I'm mostly concerned about not having a scar from my sternum down to my abdomen.

The doctors put me on morphine and go through my back with a big needle to drain five hundred cc's of blood and fluid out of my abdomen. I start to improve. They operate on my knee, put a pin in it. I still don't have a hundred percent movement in it today. But, my spleen healed. If the helicopter hadn't been there, I'd have died in the backcountry.

I didn't ski or climb for a year afterwards. The doctors said I'd never be able to ski or climb on a professional level again. I decided to take an accounting class and a computer class, to prepare for another career. That didn't last long. I got real motivated about rehabilitation, and proved those doctors wrong. I couldn't see myself ending up as an accountant or computer jock.

What did I learn from this? I learned more respect and more humility, which is a good thing, because here I was, this hot shit helicopter guide.

I learned also not to be so concerned about making nice tracks and getting face shots when I'm skiing. I learned to be a little more conservative, a little more aware of that slope.

I also learned that there really is no such thing as an "island of safety." Safety is all relative. Now, I'm always prepared for the worst. Sometimes, I'm lucky.

Appendix

Author Biographies

Erik Fair

While teaching hang gliding to hundreds of students between 1980 and 1988, Erik Fair learned that the two keys to personal safety in any thrill sport are: 1) picking the sport, and the level of involvement that is right for you; and 2) relentless risk management in the name of exceptional fun. Fair's first book, *Right Stuff for New Hang Glider Pilots,* has sold over 8,000 copies. His articles on thrill sports, recreation and fitness have appeared in The Los Angeles Times, California City Sports, SELF Magazine, Orange Coast Magazine, Soaring, Hang Gliding, Men's Fitness, and Runways magazine. Fair won the prestigious Aircraft Owners and Pilots Association 1991 Max Karant Award for Excellence in Aviation Journalism. Fair's latest book, from which his story in *No Shit* was excerpted is California Thrill Sports, published by Foghorn Press.

Ken Winkler

A teacher and writer based presently in West Los Angeles, Ken Winkler has traveled extensively throughout Asia. Winkler also works for Adventure 16, a backpacking, mountaineering and adventure travel outfitter in Southern California.

Fred and Gloria Jones

Between them, award-winning freelance writers and photographers Fred and Gloria Jones have co-authored two books (*A Climber's Guide to the High Sierra* and *The Desert Bighorn—Its Life History, Ecology and Management*); have been Field Editors for Western Boatman Magazine and Conservation Editors for Baja Explorer Magazine; have authored numerous professional publications on wildlife, natural resources, parks and recreation; have contributed many outdoor features and columns to newspapers, national and regional magazines; write copy and design brochures, booklets, fliers, advertisements and a newsletter for a large boat and travel club, Vagabundos del Mar.

Jeff Bennett

In addition to being an internationally recognized whitewater boatman, he was ranked 6th in the world at the 1991 World Rally and has paddled hundred of rivers across North and Central America. Bennett is a boating author of national repute. While his first book, *Guide to the Whitewater Rivers of Washington,* garnered recognition as Washington's best boating guide, it was his second book, *Class Five Chronicles,* from which Bennett's two stories in this book are excerpted, that vaulted Bennett into a writing class of his own. His latest book, *Rafting!* is considered by most to be the definitive guide to whitewater rafting. Bennett's books are published by his own publishing house, Swiftwater Publishing Company.

Jim Cassady

Co-author of *California Whitewater* and *Western Whitewater, From the Rockies to the Pacific,* Cassady currently resides in the San Francisco Bay area and is the founder and co-owner of Pacific River Supply in El Sobrante. Cassady has pioneered and led trips down many of the West's toughest rivers and was the designer of the SOTAR self-bailing raft and the co-designer of the Carlson River Board. Cassady has also written for the San Francisco Chronicle, Paddle Magazine, and Headwaters.

Linda Navroth

Born, raised and still living in Southern California, Linda Navroth currently works for Adventure 16 Camping Outfitters as a training manager. When not working, Navroth is fly fishing, tying flys and writing articles for the Wilderness Fly Fisher's newsletter, "Mending the Line."

Ian Black

Ian Black is a world-class boater who has paddled from Corsica to Colorado. He lives in Boulder, Colorado with his wife Brenda and serves as a managing partner for Dawg Inc., a company importing Guatemalan clothing.

Paul McHugh

Born during Hurricane King at the edge of the Florida Everglades, Paul McHugh grew up and lived there until leaving home at the age of 16 to study for the Roman Catholic priesthood for six years. McHugh completed his education at Florida State University studying literature and psychology. After graduating Summa Cum Laude he jumped on his motorcycle and traveled the U.S. looking for a place to settle. Partly because he was out of money and partly because it seemed the best place to live, McHugh ended up in Northern California where he worked as a fair hawker, custom carpenter, candle carver, masseur, commercial fisherman, logger and rancher. McHugh began writing magazine features in 1976. His first novel, *Search for Goodbye-to-Rains* was published in 1980. McHugh made environmental movies for PBS during the early '80s, serving as a producer and writer, and in 1985 was hired as chief outdoor writer for the San Francisco Chronicle—a position he has held proudly ever since.

John Long

The author of eight books, John Long's short stories have been widely anthologized and translated into many languages. His how-to books have made him a best-selling author in the outdoor/adventure industry. An internationally recognized climber/explorer, Long's first novel, *Cerro Verde,* is due out in early 1994.

Diane Christiansen

In 1973, Diane Christiansen began her adventurous lifestyle at the age of 20 by leaving the flashlight at home and, with her husband Jeff, joining the early "back to nature" movement. Their first adventure together found them walking 1,600 miles, the length of California. After graduating with a degree in Environmental Sciences and Planning, Christiansen "followed her bliss" and went to work as a professional naturalist, river guide, backpacking, climbing and sea kayaking instructor—all for schools, colleges, private outfitters and Outward Bound. Christiansen is presently the owner of her own successful consulting company, Inside/Outside Associates, and consults for non-profit groups, the media, and businesses within the outdoor adventure and recreation industry. Through her work in marketing, public relations, organizational development, and in giving motivational workshops, Christiansen draws heavily on her wealth of personal experiences (like when she got stranded on a beautiful tropical island—for cheap).

Jim Ward

Currently working as a teacher at Cuyamaca Outdoor School, a resident sixth grade outdoor science school in Southern California, Jim Ward is an avid outdoorsman who continues to enjoy pursuing the wilder side of a mountain. Formerly the editor and art director of Footprints, an award-winning quarterly newsletter distributed by Adventure 16 to over 125,000 customers/readers, Ward continues to pursue photography and art with a passion. Ward's photography has appeared in Business Week, Inc., KCET Magazine, Outside, Sierra, and Outdoor Retailer magazines. Ward's illustrations and art renderings have adorned numerous national brochures, catalogues, and educational materials. His stories, such as the one published in *No Shit,* help him to entertain his three boys, ages 12, 14, and 16.

Lynn Ferrin

Even though she has scuffed her boots on the mountains of every continent except Antarctica, Lynn Ferrin still says her main desire in life is "more boarding passes." Meanwhile, she lives in San Francisco, with her sorely neglected house plants, and slaves as editor of Motorland magazine.

Ken Hanley

Twenty three years in the adventure business, Ken Hanley is the owner/operator of Adventures Beyond, a company that conducts outdoor education outreach programs throughout the world. Hanley is the author of *The California Flytying and Fishing Guide*, published by Amato Publications, and a columnist with California Fly

Fisher Magazine and California Angler Magazine. Hanley has also been published in numerous regional and national magazines.

Peter Whittaker

Peter Whittaker is a world class climber carrying on his family's mountaineering tradition. His uncle, Jim, became the first American, in 1963, to summit Mt. Everest. His father, Lou, has led successful expeditions to Everest and Kangchenjunga, and is the co-founder and chief partner in Rainier Mountaineering, Inc., the guide service on Washington's Mt. Rainier, where Peter, now a co-owner, was introduced to climbing and guiding at the age of twelve. Peter was a member of the 1984 American Everest Expedition and the 1987 Snowbird Everest Expedition. In 1986, he founded Summits Adventure Travel, an international adventure travel company specializing in mountaineering, trekking and skiing. He has organized and led over 40 successful expeditions worldwide, including seven trips to Kilimanjaro and five trips to Aconcagua. Peter makes his home at the base of Mt. Rainier, with his wife Erika, a former member of the Austrian national ski team.

Andrea Gabbard

Andrea Gabbard is a freelance writer who divides her time between her home in the Sierra Nevada foothills and her favorite—although rapidly disappearing—Southern California beaches. As an active outdoor enthusiast, she specializes in related lifestyle topics. She is the author of several hundred articles on various aspects of the outdoors, including mountaineering, canoeing and kayaking, wildlife viewing, adventure travel and big wave surfing. In 1989, her book, *Da Bull—Life Over the Edge,* chronicled the story of pioneer big wave surfer Greg Noll. She is presently at work on the life story of Lou Whittaker, to be published in Fall '94 by The Mountaineers-Books.

Jody Foss

An adventurer in every sense of the word, Jody Foss's entry for *No Shit* is excerpted from her soon-to-be released book, *Mules Across the Great Wide Open, the True Life Adventures of Jod on the Road.*

The book chronicles her 1976 expedition riding mules from Park City, Utah to Spokane, Washington—"ninety days rockin' in the saddle, mule skinnin' ... life at three miles per hour."

Dennis Bitton

Now a freelance writer after 12 years of editing a fly fishing magazine, Dennis Bitton lives in Idaho Falls, Idaho with his wife of 27 years, Linda. They have six children and five grandchildren. Bitton is an active member of the Outdoor Writers Association of America.

John Arrington

John Arrington first donned a backpack in 1959, the summer he graduated from high school—an army rucksack no less. Arrington has gone backpacking every time he could since then. Arrington worked as a swim coach for AAU until 1983 when Wayne Gregory talked him into becoming his national sales manager. Since then, Arrington has been employed as the National Sales Manager for the Wilderness Group and also for Moonstone Mountaineering. Currently he is self employed working under contract to W.L. Gore and Associates, helping them create product knowledge seminars called the Gore-Tech Program. Arrington travels around the U.S. and Canada putting on these seminars in backcountry retailer stores. A dedicated bachelor, Arrington lives for only one woman, Tillamook Cheddar—a 12 year-old yellow Labrador retriever.

Gary Catt

Gary Catt, 47, lives peacefully in rural upstate New York. He left journalism after some 18 years of writing and editing at newspapers to work in public affairs. Catt refers to it as "going straight." He still climbs when he can—dreams when he can't. Catt insists that he needs permission from his wife and two kids to do anything and that he has turned to fishing so he won't look suspicious doing nothing.

Judging Criteria

All stories published within this book were presented to the judges anonymously and were printed on the same kind of paper in the same format and style. In this way, all entries to the *No Shit* contest were guaranteed a fair reading based entirely on writing ability, content and storyline. The judges were asked to evaluate and score each story in two categories: Entertainment Value / Compelling Storyline and Professional Crafting / Writing Quality. Each category was awarded a point total between 1 and 50 with 1 being the least favorable and 50 representing writing perfection (no, no one earned a 50, but yes, a few came close). Both scores were then totaled and each story was awarded an overall score somewhere between 2 and 100. Once each of the 4 judging magazines submitted their scores, I added up all the numbers and divided by 4 to arrive at the overall average score which represented each story's final tally. The story with the highest average score was declared the winner, next highest was awarded second prize. Numerous stories were rejected for contest entry during the initial qualifying judging round by myself and ICS publisher Tom Todd.

The judging panel involved editors and publishers from the following magazines:

Climbing — Michael Kennedy, editor and publisher
Canoe — Judy Harrison, publisher; David Harrison, editor-in-chief
Adventure West — Katrina Veit, managing editor; George Schaffer, associate editor
Women's Sports and Fitness — Jane McConnell, publisher and editor-in-chief

A very special thanks to all the judges from myself and ICS Books.

Statement Regarding Acquisition of Rights

Author Michael Hodgson and ICS Books only seek to acquire first time rights for publication of contest entrant's stories in *No Shit! There I Was...Again!* Any and all contest entrants may subsequently sell their stories to magazines, newspapers, or other publications at will. Previously published stories will also be considered. Any request for reprints from the book that involve a contestant's story will be referred directly to the contestant for negotiation.

About Michael Hodgson

Michael Hodgson is a senior editor of Adventure West Magazine, technical editor for Outdoor Retailer Magazine, and a contributing editor for Backpacker Magazine. He also pens a weekly self-syndicated equipment review column that appears in the Portland Oregonian, the San Jose Mercury News and the Salt Lake Tribune. Michael's articles have also appeared in Field and Stream, Pacific Northwest Magazine, Motorland Magazine, and The Christian Science Monitor. The author of ten books on the outdoors, Michael has been honored with numerous writing awards from the Outdoor Writers Association of America and Western Publications Association. Most recently, he was named Outdoor Writer of the Year by the Outdoor Writers Association of California.

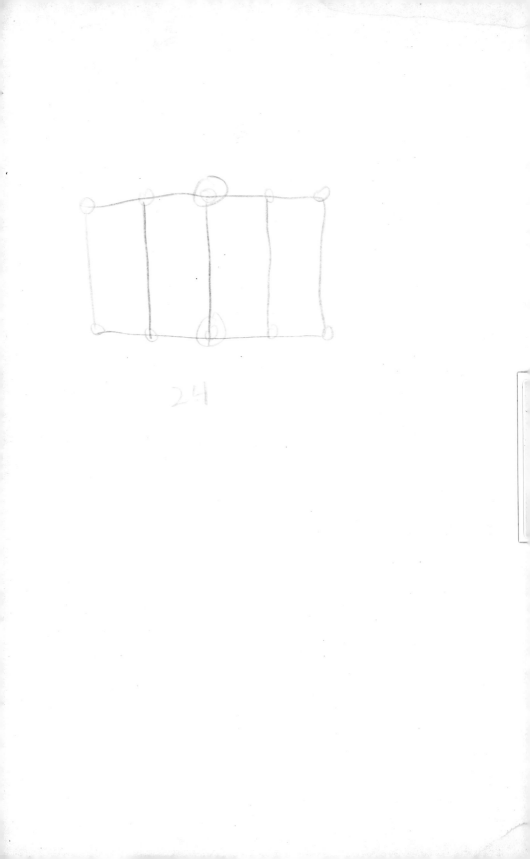

24